Developing and Spreading your Financial Tentacles

Copyright Information

Table of Content

Preface

As plants develop from seeds, and could not be without it; similarly, everyone has a humble beginning. A time when you had nothing to your name. Does it matter whether you had something or nothing in the beginning? No, it doesn't. Your current state is not a determinant of who you can be or what you can have. The point is if you have a dream or passion and you are zealous about it, you are on your way to achieve it. I know that as long as you put your whole self into achieving your goal, you would achieve that goal. While taking the small first step can make all the difference, there are two factors that can keep you from appreciating an opportunity to move forward in the days of small beginning. One is because of its apparent insignificance; second, is the initial support you can't get. But these should not deter you; a journey of a thousand miles begins with a single step.

When you achieve financial success, additional effort is required to sustain it. In all human affairs there are efforts, and there are results, and the strength of the effort is the measure of the results obtained. Any success achieve and not improved upon continually will become outdated in no distant future. What are the things to do in order to replicate your financial success?

First, continuous effort in those things that brings financial success to you; rather than strength of intelligence is the key you need to spread out your financial tentacles. Second, follow your dream or passion. Third, take risks from time to time. Forth thing to do is to get out of your comfort zone. In addition to all these, incorporate good financial management in your business. Finally, do something extra to what most people do. What is referred to as extraordinary is just a bit of extra beyond the ordinary that class you out of the many. If you must make your mark in the world of today, you must be willing to do beyond what your competitors are doing.

Welcome to your business breakthrough launch-pad session and a life beyond financial limitations!

Victor Peters - PhD

With the new day comes new strength and new thoughts.

A New Business At Its Beginning

One of the biggest challenges for entrepreneurs and small business owners is finding the funds necessary to launch their business. Financing is one of the most challenging obstacles an entrepreneur has to overcome when starting a new business. Does it matter whether you had something or nothing at the beginning? No, it doesn't. If you always base your decisions on what you have or don't have at this moment, you are never going to start; because you are limiting yourself based on your history. You become a function of your past. That's just surrendering yourself to what you had in the past, which is a very disempowering way to start. It merely serves to reinforce the status quo. Your current state is not a determinant of who you can be or what you can have. The point is that if you have a dream or passion, and you are zealous about it, you are on your way to achieving it. However, most important is your vision and ideals. Are you convinced about them?

Discover Your Vision and Ideals

Dreamers are the savior of the world. As the visible world is sustained by the invisible, so men through all their ordeals and trials are nourished by the beautiful visions of their solitary dreams. Humanity cannot forget its dreamers; it cannot let their ideals fade and die; it lives on. He who cherishes a beautiful vision, lofty ideals in his heart will one day realize it. Thomas Edison cherished a world lighted with bulbs, and he discovered it. What is your vision? Cherish your vision and ideals for out of them will grow all delightful conditions you so desired; if you remain true to them; your world would at last be built by them. To desire is to obtain, to aspire is to achieve. The greatest achievement begins as a dream and dreams are the seedlings of realities; the highest vision of the soul.

Man is made or unmade by himself; in the armory of thoughts and actions, he forges the weapons by which he destroys himself; he also fashions the tools with which he builds for himself heavenly mansions of success, joy, strength and peace. By the right choice and true application of thoughts, man builds for himself financial success, lasting harmony with his environment, and ultimate contentment; equally, by the abuse and wrong application of thoughts, he descends below the level of a beast. Between these two extremes are all the grade of characters we see; and man is the maker and master of it all. However, the thoughtless, the ignorant, and the indolent, seeing only the apparent effects of things and not the things themselves, talk of luck, fortune, and chance. Yes chance! It will always come to you at your own time. Seeing a man grow rich, they say "*How lucky he is!*" another will say "*How highly favored he is!*" One thing I have come to understand about life is that time and chance keep resurfacing themselves to mankind because nature will always work on our mind's thinking and belief. I have a few questions to ask you my reader:

1. Do you know what you want in your life?
2. Are you afraid you will be in the same financial situation you are in today a year from now?
3. Do you feel like you are not in control of your life but your life is in control of you, sending you into an unbalanced state of frustration?

Change the way you think; apply yourself to the course of positive actions. Good thoughts and actions can never produce bad results; likewise, band thoughts and actions can never produce good results. A man only begin to be a man when he ceases to be careless about the issues concerning his life, rather commences to search for the hidden justice which regulates his life. When the truth is found, and he adapts his mind to that regulating factor, he ceases to accuse others as the cause of his poor condition; instead he builds himself up in strong and definite goals of life, kick against negative circumstances, and begin to use them as aids to his rapid progress, and as a means of discovering the hidden powers and possibilities that nature has brought his way by chance. The vision you glorify in your mind, the ideal that you enthrone in your heart is what you will build your life by, and that is what you'll become someday.

Narrow Your Focus

One of the most difficult decisions in starting a small business can be what line of business to pursue. You might not be sure what talents you have that will allow you to succeed without an established company name behind you. Or you might excel in so many areas that you're not sure which one or two to pick on. In the face of all these, you need to narrow down your focus on a particular one. To make the right selection consider the following two factors as they are important guides in choosing right.

Play to Your Strengths and Interests

Ideally, you should wake up every morning feeling energetic and passionate about the work that lies ahead of you if it is your passion. At the very least, your small business idea should be something that you're interested in and that plays to your strengths. The process of figuring out what line of business to go into is not that different from figuring out what you want when you're looking for any other new job. It seems daunting because the possibilities are wide open, but that's also the main attraction of working for yourself. You don't have to limit yourself to what your resume says you're good at. What gets you excited? Don't be afraid to consider every possibility. Even the ones that don't initially seem to have any money-making potential should be given consideration.

Potential Demand for Product or Service

Is there market demand for the product or service you want to offer? Before you quit your day job for instance, you need to do some research to see if your idea has the potential to succeed. If you want to work independently as a financial planner for example, see if you can attract clients based on your existing credentials and experience. If you want to offer a product, then you will want to start doing market research, product testing and surveys. It can be hard to find the time to pursue your own business while you're still working for someone else, but it's the most secure way to test your idea without taking a big financial risk. And if you're not motivated enough to find the time for it, maybe you're not really that interested in becoming a small business owner.

Have a Business Plan

For a new business at its beginning, a lot of planning is required and it takes a lot of momentum to get started; therefore have an operational business plan. If you are not sure what this entails, it is wise to seek advice from successful entrepreneurs around you. Own your success right from the beginning; build a business plan and work it each day. According to free encyclopedia, a plan is typically any diagram or list of steps with timing and resources, used to achieve an objective. A plan is about action. Successful businessmen and individuals not only know their plan, but they track it, measure it, review it and live by it. First thing is to get a notebook, or any blank document and list out what you need to get accomplished in your business over a period of time: e.g. in a month, in three months, in six month or a year. This may include any appointments or meetings you may have. Secondly, create a timetable for yourself. At what time should you be done with the first objective on your list? List each activity, starting with the earliest one, and working your way through the time and schedules for accomplishing each of the objectives. Make sure that you work around any appointments or meetings you have. Of course, everyone's days are different, so each person's plan should be different. Finally, it is important to take a moment after each allotted amount of time to review how productive you were during that time. Did you manage to cover everything you needed to get done? If yes, good effort, keep it up; if no you will have to give yourself some few minutes to reorganize--close your eyes and relax. This way you will be able to effectively transit into the next activity you have to do.

The flip side to being focused is having no focus at all. A lot of people don't achieve success generally in life simply because they don't make any decision. As you have set a plan of what to accomplish within a given time frame, stick to your plan and gradually get each of the objectives executed to completion one after the other. Refuse to be distracted by external forces that may want to disrupt your plan.

Have Working Marketing Strategies

When you explore different marketing strategies, you will see that not all of them works like you hoped. Don't just dump your marketing plans because results were not what you thought they would be. Keep them aside for now; and execute the one that you think is viable. At times some of these strategies will do well at different times. Just like getting a race car to peak performance is a matter of sharpening in on the perfect settings, so too is a good, comprehensive marketing strategy. Picking target markets, picking offers, picking messages, call to actions and frequencies are parts of the marketing machine. Watch your reports, see what's working and what isn't, and rather than scrap your racing machine because it's got a tire running flat, fix that one problem, and get back on the track. So take advantage of marketing that allows you to focus in on particular target audiences. If your best customers are females from age twenty-five to forty-five, don't spend your money marketing a program that's going to be seen by everyone. If your business only serves one particular town, or a part of a town, buying regional or national advertisement doesn't make much sense. If you combine the two scenarios I just listed, the right solution would be to find a way to market to females twenty-five to forty-five who live in your town.

If you are marketing to the right people in the right place, you can control your spending and also have high percentage of response from contacted customers. In this case, your effort yields better results. You want to be specific as to places where you put money, because if you say the right things to the right people in your marketing, they will have a higher chance of responding. This means you get more return on your marketing investment. That's a great thing!

We are all taught that selling benefits is better than selling features. In lion share of situations, this is certainly true. However, more powerful than simply selling benefits and linking them to features, is to sell the ideal. The ideal is the thing or the experience that your customer is looking for. For example, if you have a travel agency, your customers might appreciate the benefit of saving money, and they like the thought of that. When doing marketing, it is important we make sure that while we are listing our benefits, we also remember to address the ideal.

Good Customer Relationship Management

A business that will go places will from the beginning ensure good relationship with customers. It costs six to seven times more to acquire a new customer than to keep an existing one. Money can't buy one of the most important things you need to promote in your business, that is, relationship. How do customer relationships drive your business? It's all about finding people who believe in your products and/or services. Powerful relationships don't just happen from one-time meetings at networking events; or another pocketful of random business cards that litters your desk. What you need is a plan to make those connections grow and work for you. Successful businesses have journeyed the way of Customer Relationship Management (CRM) for several years to a point where they now know that no customers no business. CRM is the practices, strategies and technologies that companies use to manage; record and evaluate customer interactions in order to compel sales growth by deepening and enriching relationships with their customer bases.

Loyal customers are the best salespeople. Your business may just be starting; and all you have are just few customers. What you do with the little determines what the size will look like in the future. So spend the time to build your network and do the follow-up. Today there are cost effective tools, like e-mail marketing, that make this easy. You can e-mail a simple newsletter, an offer or an update message of interest to your network (make sure it's of interest to them, not just to you). Then they'll remember you and what you do and deliver value back to you with referrals. They'll hear about opportunities you'll never hear about. The only way they can say, "Wow, I met somebody who's really good at ABC office today; is to give them a call. Such customers become your sales force.

Creating and nurturing a strong relationship with a customer is key to the ongoing success of a business, especially a young business for that matter. A strong customer relationship not only means that the client is likely to keep doing business with a company over the long-term, it also means that the chances of that customer recommending the company and its products to others are greatly enhanced. So identify customer needs and wants. This is accomplished by employing the dual processes of interacting with the client while also making use of background research. Using both approaches makes it possible to meet identified needs while anticipating future needs and presenting the customer with a solution before there is a chance for the client to look elsewhere.

Provide full disclosure where and when necessary, especially when interacting with a client. This means focusing on providing a complete answer in response to customers' queries and concerns. Be honest in those communications and set reasonable expectations for getting back to clients if you need to do some research before making a response. Doing so leaves the impression that what the customer thinks matters greatly and that the customer is in fact your priority.

Seek customer feedback promptly. This includes seeking suggestions on new features or products that would interest the customer, as well as evaluation of current products and features. Always listen carefully and respond in a manner that lets the client know you understand the suggestions or critiques that have been offered. Thank the client even if the comments are negative.

Getting Started and Goal Setting

The magnitude of your beginning is not that important when a new business is concerned; but rather the progress you are making each passing day from the first day of these days of small beginning is more crucial. Of all striking truth pertaining to small scale business development which has been researched and brought to light in this age, none is more fruitful and result-oriented than the fact that in starting new business; wisdom, knowledge and insight, are essential because these are unarguably what you need to get the business started and sustained on the part of success. The key to business success is having access to insight. An insight you discover, opens the door of opportunities to you. It is only by much searching and mining that gold and diamond are obtained; and man can find every truth connected with his life if he is willing to dig deep into the mine of his soul.

Power of Positive Thinking

The thoughts that we repeatedly think shape our lives. In order to make changes in our life, we have to make changes in our thinking process. It is necessary to change our thoughts. It is like ejecting a DVD and inserting a new one that we like better. The new mental DVD will in time, change our behavior, actions and attitude, and attract into our lives people, situations and events corresponding with our new thoughts. One single thought is not strong enough to make a change, but if the same thought is repeated often, it gradually gains strength.

A thought that is often repeated takes root in the subconscious mind, and from there, it affects our lives and even our environment. The great thing about this process is that we don't need to strain or overexert ourselves to make it happen. All we have to do is to choose a thought that we want to come true, and keep repeating it.

You can overcome negative habits and build new ones, develop new skills and abilities, and even change your circumstances and attain anything that you truly desire. The power of thoughts can help you get a new job, improve your relationships, earn more money or improve your life. All this does not happen overnight. It needs time, and depends on how sincere you are in your efforts, and on how much time and focus you put into your new way of thinking. This is mental work, but this does not mean that you stay passive and wait for things to happen. You need to keep an open mind and be willing to take action when necessary. Decide what you want to get or achieve, and start thinking about it often during the day, or at several specific times during the day. These repeated thoughts would ultimately get stronger, and bring inner and outer changes. The power of thoughts is a real power. Thought become things. You have certainly used it many times without realizing it. When you know how it works and how to use it consciously, you gain the ability to transform, improve and master your life.

People who have entertained negative thoughts and feelings most of their lives, expect failure and do not feel worthy of success. If they have experienced lack and hardships, they believe that success is not for them. In these cases, everything associated with success might evoke negative feelings. Your thoughts and feelings can draw or repel success. They shape your beliefs and expectations about success or failure. Thoughts too often, come and go and change direction like the wind. They influence your mind the same way that the wind affects the direction of a flag. One moment the flag may be fluttering this way, and a moment later in a different direction. One moment you might be thinking one thing or see things from a certain viewpoint, and a moment later this can change.

When your thoughts, feelings and moods become steady and under your control, your life also becomes under your control. You become the deciding factor, not the outside influences or passing moods. In order to control your thoughts, feelings and moods and navigate your life, concentration and willpower need to be developed. Concentration and willpower constitute the steering wheel of your life, with which you can navigate the boat of your life toward success and achievement.

Your predominant, habitual thoughts and feelings determine whether you will achieve success or not, and whether you will feel satisfied upon realization or not. This means that you have to be more aware of your thoughts and feelings. It is important to learn to be more positive, less critical, and less worried. Then, when success is achieved, you can enjoy the happiness of achievement. Thoughts, attitudes and habits can be changed. The change does not come overnight. Some inner work is necessary. Positive thoughts and feelings make you happier and more receptive to success, and a positive disposition bestows upon you the ability to enjoy success when it comes.

Take it as a challenge, and pay more attention to your thoughts and feelings. Find out what kind of thoughts you think and what kind of feelings you usually experience in connection with them. If your thoughts and feelings are positive that's okay. However, if you think and feel failure, unhappiness and dissatisfaction, then you need to do something about this. Why is it that people desire success? There is a desire for growth in each one of us. It is the cosmic desire for expression and expansion. This desire manifests in every form of life. We see it everywhere, even in a blade of grass, which can grow on a rock or on a wall. The desire for success is the inner natural desire for growth, expansion and expression.

The Strength of your Desire

The strength of your desire determines if your business will ultimately takeoff or not. It decides the level of results you'll also get. Most people admire and respect strong individuals, who have won great success by manifesting willpower and strong desires. Willpower is the inner strength that makes it possible to make a decision and follow it through, take action, handle and execute any plan or task until it is accomplished, regardless of inner and outer resistance, discomfort or difficulties. Willpower bestows the ability to overcome laziness, temptations and negative habits, and to carry out actions, even if they require effort, they are unpleasant and tedious, or are contrary to one's habits. They admire people, who improved their life, learned new skills, overcame difficulties and hardships or rise high in their chosen field. The truth is that everyone can reach high levels of willpower and strength of mind, through a practical method of training. These skills are not reserved for a few special people.

Getting rid of fear is very important, so that your desire may have full strength with which to work. In order to attract a thing it is necessary that the mind should fall in love with it, and be conscious of its existence, almost to the exclusion of everything else. You must get in love with the thing you wish to attain, just as much as you would if you were to meet the girl or man you wished to marry. I do not mean that you should lose interest in everything else in the world - that won't do, for the mind must have recreation and change. But, what I mean is that you must be so "set" upon the desired thing that all else will seem of secondary importance. A man in love may be pleasant to everyone else, and may go through the duties and pleasures of life with good spirit, but underneath it all he is humming to himself "Just One Girl;" and every one of his actions is bent toward getting that girl, and making a comfortable home for her. Do you see what I mean? You must get in love with the thing you want, and you must get in love with it in earnest. That is a strong desire. A man or woman in search of success must first make what he desired his ruling passion - he must keep his mind on the main chance. Success is jealous - that's why we speak of her as feminine. She demands a man's whole affection, and if he begins flirting with other fair charmers, she soon turns her back upon him. If a man allows his strong interest in the main chance to be sidetracked, he will be the loser. Mental force operates best when it is concentrated. You must give your best and most earnest thought to what you desire. Just as the man who is thoroughly in love will think out plans and schemes whereby he may please the fair one, so will the man who is in love with his work or business give it his best thought, and the result will be that a hundred and one plans will come into his field of consciousness, many of which are very important. The mind works on the subconscious plane, remember, and almost always along the lines of the ruling passion or desire. It will fix up things, and patch together plans and schemes.

Everyone is constantly confronted and tempted by an endless stream of desires and distractions, many of which are not really important, useful or of any real value. By learning to refuse to satisfy every one of them, you get stronger. Rejecting, and refusing to satisfy useless, harmful or unnecessary desires and actions, sharpen and strengthen your inner strength, that gives your desire a boost. By constant practice, your inner power grows, just like exercising your muscles at a gym increases your physical strength. In both cases, when you need inner power or physical strength, they are available at your disposal. It is your desires, beliefs, thoughts and actions that get you over and constantly above obstacles in the pursuit of your desire. If you desire something strong enough in your mind and long enough, nature will begin to line these things up to make it happen. It is a natural principle. You will become as small as your controlling desire; and as great as your dominant aspiration. To desire is to obtain and to aspire is to achieve. Have a strong desire for the kind of success you want and it will come your way.

Believe in Yourself

If you have been strike down long enough by negative forces of life and even people around you, believing in yourself can seem impossible. When you have had people in your life who do not boost you up when you needed such support, you may have concluded that it cannot get better anymore. You proceed to discount your skills and abilities based on what other people have said. You are doing a great disservice to yourself and giving your power to someone else. To reach your goals in life, believing in yourself is extremely important if you want to get anywhere. Those assumptions about who you are become a way of life.

You will stay stuck in these patterns until you change the way you think. Fear is the greatest opposition against you believing in yourself. Fear is the parent of worry, hate, jealousy, malice, anger, discontentment, failure and all the rest. The best way to overcome the habit of fear is to assume the mental attitude of courage, just as the best way to get rid of darkness is to let in light. It is a waste of time to fight a negative thought-habit by recognizing its force and trying to deny it out of existence by mighty efforts. The best, surest, easiest and quickest method is to assume the existence of positive thought desired in its place; and by constantly dwelling upon the positive thought, manifest it into objective reality.

A man who rids himself of fear will find that the rest of his worries have disappeared. The only way to be free is to get rid of fear. I regard the conquest of fear as the first important step to be taken by those who wish to exercise a strong believe in themselves. So long as fear masters you, you are in no condition to make progress in the realm of self-confidence, and I must insist that you start to work at once to get rid of this obstruction. You can do it - if you only go about it in earnest. And when you have ridded yourself of the vile thing, life will seem entirely different to you - you will feel happier, freer, stronger, more positive, and will be more successful in every undertaking of life. There are few things you can practice to aid your self-confidence.

Try Even When You Think You Can't Do It: Make a vow to yourself today that you will try your best at any opportunity that comes your way. It does not matter if you have fallen on your face before or whether you think it's even possible. The important thing is to pledge to yourself that you will try no matter what the outcome may be. The worst thing to do to yourself is to assume you can't do it before even trying. Tell yourself right now that any effort to do better is not a waste of your precious time.

Establish Evidence For The Assumptions: Get some paper and start a list. List every one of those things you really believe about yourself that you can do and those things you think you cannot do. List them whether they are large or small. Once you have that list go through each assumption and examine it. Ask yourself, "Is this true? What is the proof?" Then go and do whatever it is you feel you cannot. It does not matter if you do it better than anyone else. It only matters that you do.

Never Give Up: Even though you have tried and failed this should not deter you. Success requires effort and continuous improvement. So try out those things again and again. Challenge the situation and have an open mind to the possibility that you could be wrong! The power of belief is astounding, even to the point of the miraculous. There are some cases where even the seemingly impossible occurs due to the power of belief. With every success, whether large or small, the belief in yourself will grow. That will be the push you need to keep stepping outside your comfort zone and attain the accomplishments you truly deserve.

Set your Goals

Goal setting is a powerful process for thinking about your ideal future, and for motivating yourself to turn your vision of this future into reality. The process of setting goals helps you choose where you want to go in life. By knowing precisely what you want to achieve, you know where you have to concentrate your efforts. You'll also quickly spot the distractions that can, so easily, lead you astray. In developing a strong financial future appropriate goal setting is essential.

Identifying and setting clear, achievable goals is a crucial part of anyone's financial growth plan. A financial success goal is the exact time-dependent schedule of what is to be achieved over a period of time. For instance, in the next five years I plan to take my business to a level of total asset amounting to US$10 million. Of course, the business may be currently at a total asset capacity of US$300,000. Making the goal precise helps you determine how much effort you need to put in to get your goal accomplished. And on a pre-determined time interval within the period of the goal-setting, an appraisal is done to check if progress is being recorded or not.

There are three types of goals: short-term, mid-term, and long-term. Short-term goals are to be met in one year or less; mid-term goal is scheduled for between one to five years and long-term goal is for five years or more. For instance, vacations, gifts, and electronics are typical short-term goals. A down payment for a house is a common mid-term goal. Long-term goals may include business growth and development, saving for retirement and a child's higher education.

Tracking your goals is essential. The Financial Goals Chart will help determine the timeline for your goals and the amount of money you'll need to regularly set aside in order to reach them. You may find the numbers daunting or even not realistic based on your current financial situation. You may be able to increase your income and/or decrease your expenses or have to consider adjusting your goals. Determining your priorities is essential. If you share your finances with someone else, discuss and set priorities together. It is not uncommon for couples to work at cross-purposes financially without even knowing it. By communicating with each other and determining what's most important, it will be much easier to reach your goals.

Taking stock of what your financial situation is today can help you determine what you need to do tomorrow. Are you on the right track or do you need to make changes? Do you know exactly where your money is going each month? If not, you are not alone. Many people are well aware of the symptoms of financial distress being experienced, such as having credit card debt, overdrawing a checking account, not being able to save, or paying bills late, but are not sure of the cause. Assessing your cash flow can help you figure that out.

Incomes are cash in-flows. The most common source of income is wages from a job, but it can also include things like investment earnings, child support, allowance, rental payments (if you are a landlord), government benefits, gifts, and profits from self-employment or a hobby. While gifts, child support, and some government benefits are generally not taxable, most income is. Your gross income is your income before taxes are taken out. Your net income is your income after taxes are taken out.

Expenses are cash out-flows. They can include essentials, such as mortgage or rent, food, and medical costs, as well as things you choose to spend money on, such as piano lessons and vacation. Savings can be considered an expense too – the money may not be leaving your hands, but you are setting it aside, and not to be used for other purposes.

Cash flow software can be used to list your income and expenses; and get accurate figures on where your money is going mostly. If your income exceeds your expenses, you have a positive cash flow. If your expenses exceed your income, you have a negative cash flow.

3

Building your Financial Base from Small Beginning

As plants develop from seeds, and could not be without it; so is every action of man that springs from the hidden seeds of thought in his mind. Action is the budding of thoughts, and joy and suffering are its fruits; thus does a man rewarded depending on which choice he makes for himself. A seed of corn buried inside the soil soon germinates and grow into plants that can bring forth two to three hubs with each containing hundreds of grains. A journey of a thousand miles begins with a single step.

The Seed of Small Beginning

What most people believe is to get somebody like an uncle, brother, sister, father or a friend to provide them with huge sums of money in order to prosper. This system creates dependency syndrome in the society. You need to know that wealth accumulation is a gradual process. You have to start from class one and graduate at the end. People who want to jump the queue by resorting to stealing and drug trafficking in order to get rich quick tend to be the losers. You need to go by the ant way to achieve financial success through financial wisdom. The tiny creature does not consume all its food but saves some for the future.

Always do your best. What you plant now, you will harvest later.

Does it matter whether you had something or nothing in the beginning? No, it doesn't. If you always base your decisions on what you have or don't have at this moment, you are never going to get far; because you are limiting yourself based on your history. You become a function of your past. You also become a shadow of your past as well. That's just surrendering yourself to what you had in the past, which is a very disempowering way to live. It merely serves to reinforce the status quo. Your current state is not a determinant of who you can be or what you can have. Remember, you have unlimited power in you. Focus on your WHAT, not your HOW. The point is if you have a dream or passion and you are committed to working it, you are on your way to achieve it. I know that as long as you put your whole self into achieving your goal, you would achieve that goal. It doesn't matter what you have or what you don't have. If there is something you have that could help to achieve the goal – then great, you would leverage on it to achieve your goal. If there is nothing, then sure, you would just figure out how to get it, or if it is not possible to get it – create it yourself. People may nurse fear about you achieving your goal, don't be bordered; their fears are mere projections of themselves than of your belief. In your mind, it should be plainly clear. The outcome is fixed. The question is merely how to get there.

While taking the small first step can make all the difference, there are two factors that can keep you from appreciating an opportunity to move forward. One is because of its apparent insignificance; we may not even recognize the small beginning that's available to us. Second, is the initial support you can't get.

I remember a friend who left a well-paying salesman job to enter a doctoral program. Though Andrew had long wanted to pursue this goal, he assumed it was financially impossible, since he was a married man with children and in his forties. Finally he faced up to the fact that there was a small beginning he could make, which was to apply for grants. He made six applications, assuming his prospects for success were minimal. To his astonishment, four of the six were granted. When Andrew shared this personal triumph with me, I couldn't help but think of how many people out there, who needed this same financial assistance and would qualify for it, yet have concluded that it isn't worth the trouble to apply. Andrew himself had overlooked this option for years. So don't despise chances of small beginnings. Of course, writing a grant application means some uninspiring paper work, and this suggests a second factor that can keep us from recognizing the chance to make a small beginning--the fact that we may look with contempt upon what we have to do.

A typical rich man accumulates wealth starting from zero. In '*The Millionaires Mind*, the author noted in his research that over 90% of the millionaires he studied in America were first generations. That is to say they started creating wealth from the scratch. All that a potential rich person needs to start with is financial wisdom. He knows that if he could raise $1 today, He could double it tomorrow and triple it within the next three days. He does not despise little things. When the rich comes across a penny, he bows, thank God and picks it up because a little drop of water makes a mighty ocean. He is always grateful to the little things that come his way. He does not rush to get rich because "*Rome was not built in a day*".

The rich does not eat his seed but sows it and wait patiently for it to mature. He spends time and energy to take good care of the seed. The seed would continue to regenerate some more fruits for him to enjoy for the rest of his life. So he does not need to grow any more seed. Wealth creation is like education. You need to start from class one and pursue to the university level depending on your performance. You cannot start from class 4 or 6. People who start creating wealth from class 4 without having financial wisdom face a lot of problems. Many a time they are unable to sustain their wealth. For this reason, the rich teaches his children about wealth creation so that he can pass on the wealth from one generation to another.

When we look carefully at the path leading to personal success, we often realize that it began with a modest step forward, that in time reaped a much greater harvest than we anticipated. With the eyes of hindsight, we look back to such starting efforts with awe and gratitude. We realize there was greatness in that moment of small beginning that we didn't begin to appreciate at that time. We may tremble, too, to think of how close we came to not taking that one initial step that opened such important doors.

Have a Plan

Own your success; build a plan and work it each day. According to free encyclopedia, a plan is typically any diagram or list of steps with timing and resources, used to achieve an objective. A plan is about action. Successful individuals not only know their plan, but they track it, measure it, review it and live by it. First thing is to get a notebook, or any blank document and list out what you need to get accomplished over that period of time: e.g. in a month, in three months, in six month or a year. This may include any appointments or meetings you may have. Secondly, create a timetable for yourself. At what time should you be done with the first objective on your list? List each activity, starting with the earliest one, and working your way through the time and schedules for accomplishing each of the objectives. Make sure that you work around any appointments or meetings you have. Of course, everyone's days are different, so each person's plan should be different. Finally, it is important to take a moment after each allotted amount of time to review how productive you were during that time. Did you manage to cover everything you needed to get done? If yes, good effort, keep it up; if no you will have to give yourself some few minutes to reorganize--close your eyes and relax. This way you will be able to effectively transit into the next activity you have to do.

The flip side to being focused is having no focus at all. A lot of people don't achieve success generally in life simply because they don't make any decision. As you have set a plan of what to accomplish within a given time frame, stick to your plan and gradually get each of the objectives executed to completion. Refuse to be distracted by external forces that may want to disrupt your plan.

Capitalize on your Strengths and Interests

Main key to fulfillment in life is to recognize and make the most out of your "core strengths." Your core strength may equally be seen as your talent. If you figure out what you are best at doing, and take advantage of these skills, a rewarding life will follow. The creator has never created beings of useless purpose. While you were yet in the belly of your mother he has designed you for a purpose. Therefore, everyone has a range of abilities; but the things that we do just because we are good at them, or because other people value them, may not be the things that make us happy anyway. These strengths are simply a means to an end. True fulfillment comes from building our lives on our core strengths and interests, the ones we most enjoy doing.

But how do you start to identify these specific abilities among all the tasks you complete every day? One good way is to ask yourself a series of open-ended questions such as:

- What do I love doing?
- What am I often complimented for?

- When am I at my happiest moment and what was I doing then?
- What makes me unique, in each area of life?
- Try completing these sentences: "I am really good at...", "I find it easy to...", "When faced with a challenge, the way I approach it is...", "The talents that I use are..."

Sometimes you could get a lead from your friends, family and colleagues by asking them where they believe your strengths lies. It is possible they think you already know, so tell them to give you a candid answer. Ask them: "What do you value most about me?" "What is the most interesting thing about me you like?" "What do you think my strengths are?" The answers to these questions will give you a good idea of where your core strengths and passions lie. These skills can be practical, such as computer programming, organizing people, and events co-ordination; or less tangible, such as the ability to make people laugh. You can then focus your attention on the results, the core strengths that make you unique and can help you achieve great success and fulfillment.

Core strengths generally can be classified into three key areas: play, personal and work. But of the three, the personal area is fundamental. It might include confidence, generosity, energy, compassion, or honesty. These comprise the background of every activity you undertake. The work area does not simply means paid employment, but all purposeful activity such as money management, housekeeping, or volunteer work. Strengths in this area may include organization and planning, time management, leadership or problem-solving. In the play area, your strengths may include sporting talents such as football, table tennis, badminton; or creative abilities, competitiveness, or social factors such as being a great host and putting people at their ease, or allowing others to open up and share their problems.

To identify your core strength, look for common ideas across all areas of your life. Doing so, you may also identify some weaknesses. An awareness of these also is valuable, but for the time being just focus on the positive aspects, those that give you pleasure. To be truly happy, life coaches recommend that your top qualities are reflected and developed across your working life and leisure time.

Successful people capitalize on their strengths and avoid putting pressure on their weaknesses. But how best do you bring your core strengths to the forefront of your life? A career change is one way, but there are less radical changes you can make too. Such changes include:

- When possible, say no to tasks that do not play to your strengths and interest. Please know that your weaknesses are someone else's talents. So look for your own talents.
- Take a bold step by bringing one of your personal strengths to work or play. For example, your family life may benefit from some of the cheerfulness you show at work.
- Keep taking small steps until there are visible positive changes.
- Let go of activities you don't enjoy. Anything which you approach with a feeling of anxiety, after a long period of procrastination, is not playing to your core strengths, so delegate when you can.
- Aim to spend the majority of your time on your core strengths.

- Cultivate relationships with those who supports you, it shows curiosity, and make you feel enthusiastic.

- Choose one of your top talents and extend it right out of your comfort zone. For example, if you love to entertain and have a friend who loves planning, how about organizing a large charity dinner?

The price to pay for wasting and ignoring your talents usually is a life of frustration, regret and missed opportunities. One such life is described with terrifying accuracy in Kazuo Ishiguro's novel *Remains of the Day*, a motivating read if you should need one. Your talents are unique — nothing can take them away. But they will fade with time if they are ignored. The more you choose to honor and develop your special gifts, the more you enhance every aspect of your own life as well as the lives of the people around you.

Build Up Your Self-Confidence

The way we feel about ourselves greatly influences how we live. Self-confidence is a tool you can use in your everyday life to manage your fears and become able to do more of the things that really matter to you. However, not many people realize that their self-confidence works just like the human muscle - it grows in response to the level of performance you engage it. Either you use it or you lose it.

According to Dr. John Eliot, confidence is not a guarantee of success, but a pattern of thinking that will improve your likelihood of success, it is a tenacious search for ways to make things work. This means that we will be OK regardless of the ups and downs we have in life temporarily.

Self-confidence is extremely important in almost every aspect of our lives, yet so many people struggle to find it. Sadly, this can be a vicious circle: people who lack self-confidence can find it difficult to become successful. Confident people inspire confidence in others: their audience, their peers, their bosses, their customers, and their friends. And gaining the confidence of others is one of the key ways in which a self-confident person finds success. The good news is that self-confidence really can be learned and built on. And, whether you're working on your own self-confidence or building the confidence of other people around you, it's well-worth the effort!

Friends, look into building your self-confidence. As long as you keep on stretching yourself enough, you'll find your self-confidence building up rapidly. What's more, you'll have earned your self-confidence - because you'll have put in the hard graft necessary to be successful! Self-confidence is not related to ability, yet rather to our own expectations of ourselves. If we can focus on our own expectations, rather than what we think others have for us, we will be OK with whatever results we achieve. Goal setting is unarguably the most important skill you can learn to improve your self-confidence. I have made this point clear at the beginning of this book. Setting goal and sticking to your goal improve your self-worth. We gain a sense of self-worth when we see ourselves mastering skills and achieving goals that matter in those skill areas. This is what build-up confidence in us and makes us to believe that if we learn and work hard in a particular area, we'll succeed; and it's this type of confidence that leads people to accept difficult challenges, and persist in the face of setbacks. You need this attributes to succeed financially.

Some people believe that self-confidence can be built with affirmations and positive thinking. I believe that there is some truth in this; but it is equally important to build self-confidence by setting and achieving goals - thereby building competence. Without this underlying competence, you don't have self-confidence: you have shallow over-confidence, with all of the issues, upset and failure that this brings.

Overall, make a clear and unequivocal promise to yourself that you are absolutely committed to your goals, and that you will do all in your power to achieve them. If as you're doing it, you find doubts starting to surface write them down and challenge them calmly and rationally. If they dissolve under scrutiny, that's great. However if they are based on genuine risks, make sure you set additional goals to manage these appropriately.

Financing your Business

Financing your business is one of the most critical components to achieving overall success. Creating and sustaining your own business isn't just a way to create wealth – it's a way to pursue your life's dreams and find personal fulfillment. This path isn't an easy one, but it's one that all of history's greatest entrepreneurs have had to follow. Though starting a business is easier if you have vast reserves of cash, it's possible to build a successful business from the ground up with smartness, perseverance, and dedication even if you aren't loaded. If you're prepared to work hard and learn from your failures, you have the once-in-a-lifetime chance of building a successful business you can proudly call your own.

To start with, if you are on a job; keep your current job. By retaining a reliable source of income, you save yourself from the worry of not knowing how you'll pay your bills and from dealing with mountains of potential debt. Ideally, when your new business begins to pick up steam, you can gradually make the transition from a full time employee at your old job to a consultant or part–time worker. Eventually, you can transfer to your own business full–time. Though in real life this process often doesn't go quite as smoothly as we think, but it's almost always safer than dropping everything to pursue a dream that hasn't materialized yet. If you are using personal or family funds to finance a business it is called Boot Strapping the business. Boot strapping can involve personal investment by the founders, their family and friends and/or the owners foregoing salary. It is wise for every business owner to have at least some personal funds at risk since that shows other potential investors that you are committed to the success of the business.

In line with the objective of this book, emphasis is more on readers who are starting off with little or no capital. One of the ways for such individual is by participating in a Business Plan Competition (BPC). Seek for information on places where such competitions are taking place. In the competitions, you present your business idea and plan before a panel of judges who will determine the winner(s). Depending upon the particular contest, you may receive a substantial sum of money, and even if you don't win, you will get great pointers on running the business.

Option two is Business Incubation (BI). Business Incubation is also useful for businesses that are starting up and can't afford secretarial support and other necessities for handling office functions. Comprehensive support for hatchling businesses in the form of reduced rent, flexible space, shared services, access to professional services and an environment of energy and entrepreneurial spirit are commonly found in business incubators. However, this may not be available in all parts of the world.

Option three is to engage in a menial job to raise some startup capital. The amount may be very small, never mind don't despise the days of small beginning. Instead put courage into what you are doing and remain focus from the beginning. If you have a plan all you need do is to check through your plan and see how best you can start with the little you have.

Option four is to form Strategic Partnerships (SP) with people of trusted integrity who has some funds to inject into the business. A note of warning here, this partnership should be well documented. Never go into any partnership with anyone without paper reference or agreement backing up the business; and how the profits will be shared both now and in the distant future. The paper aspect is necessary because of any need to approach court of law for claims in the future. Another way is if your partner has links with companies; the company will support by bringing valuable industry expertise, resources, and/or bargaining power to your new business.

Handling Disappointment

Don't let today's disappointments cast a shadow on tomorrow's dreams. Disappointment generally is one of life's most uncomfortable moment, and no one like to witness it on regular basis. It is complex, and containing a subset of other emotions like anger, hurt, sadness, and probably many others too subtle to identify. Sometimes, those emotions by themselves are easier to deal with, but disappointments can leave you at a slack end. In most cases, it happens in a particular area of our life, but the negative emotion soon quickly take over our entire life; that if not properly handled may lead to just anything negative you can imagine.

Pain and suffering are the soil of strength and courage.

Kennedy was a retired military officer who served his country meritoriously for thirty five years. His pension was delayed for about six years after retirement. He had the assurance that once his retirement benefits are paid he will at least be financially comfortable as an average citizen. Over the six years of waiting he had borrowed money from individuals and banks to meet his immediate needs; with the promise to pay back once his pension is fully paid. After a few months into the sixth year, there was an announcement that all retirees will be paid their gratuity in a couple of weeks. So he was happy that at last all he borrowed would be paid back. They were told to appear at a bank in a week's time for the payment. Just two days to the said time, there was a change of government in that country and the payment could not proceed as planned. On hearing the news,

Kennedy was terribly disappointed; and he committed suicide because he was greatly in debt. Handling disappointment is a way to avoid complete breakdown when you are at your low end. In this book, I have discussed three principal ways to handle disappointments among many others. I believe they will assist you in getting out of this emotional incarceration easily.

Let It Out: One of the hardest things to do in a world where everything is immediate, everyone is under external pressure, and time is a scarce resource; is to allow negative experience or circumstances around you. Even at the most difficulties times, such as grieving, on average we only allow ourselves 1 to 2 weeks off work, and then we mostly expect to get back into normality again. We human beings are not very good at allowing the experience of negative emotions to go that soon. The only time we have this ability in its purest sense is when we were young children who have yet to be told or taught what is socially acceptable. Children will tantrum and cry and scream, or laugh until it runs out and they are genuinely ready to move on.

Genuinely experiencing emotions, no matter how painful it may be, is one of the beauties of life but we should be aware that we need to get over it as soon as possible to avoid collateral damage to our life. So let it go early and move on with your life. If you get hooked up with that disappointment for a long time, good things may pass without you noticing it.

Know Your Own Heart: Disappointment can ripple through to the core of who you are if you do not properly manage it. If you don't know what your core values are, you may not have a framework to support you when you experience negative emotions. For example, one of my core values is open-heartedness. I wish to keep an open heart and be ready to share love and kindness with others, irrespective of how they might behave. I would like to always try to choose to act with love and kindness towards others, rather than with negativity. When someone disappoints me and I feel like closing and withdrawing, I remember this core value, then pause and make a choice. I wish to be an open-hearted person. These negative feelings are thoughts, and they will pass away. Do I choose to remain open-hearted, or do I choose to follow the easier instinct and close off? More often than not, I choose to be in line with my values over the automatic response to the situation. It doesn't happen every single time, but most. Knowing your own heart and your values gives you the freedom of choice. You can choose to be driven by what happens to you, or you can choose to live in line with your principles. The latter has helped me to overcome disappointments and negative situations in a healthy way. The challenge of disappointment allows me to practice living closer to my values, and stops me from being swallowed up by it.

Practice Advance Forgiveness: Advance forgiveness means forgiving whosoever brought disappointment to you even before the disappointment occurs. It is one of the best ways to live your live to the fullest. You will find out that over the time the disappointment ligers in your mind you rub yourself of joy, peace and tranquility; and make room for other negative emotions like anger, hurt, sadness, and probably many others as mentioned above.

Perseverance and Self-Determination

In building a strong financial base, persistence and self-determination are two important companions on your way to achieving your goal. It is pretty clear that self-determination, an inner strength is the ability to proceed and carry out specific plans and actions despite internal resistance, external obstacles, and discomfort.

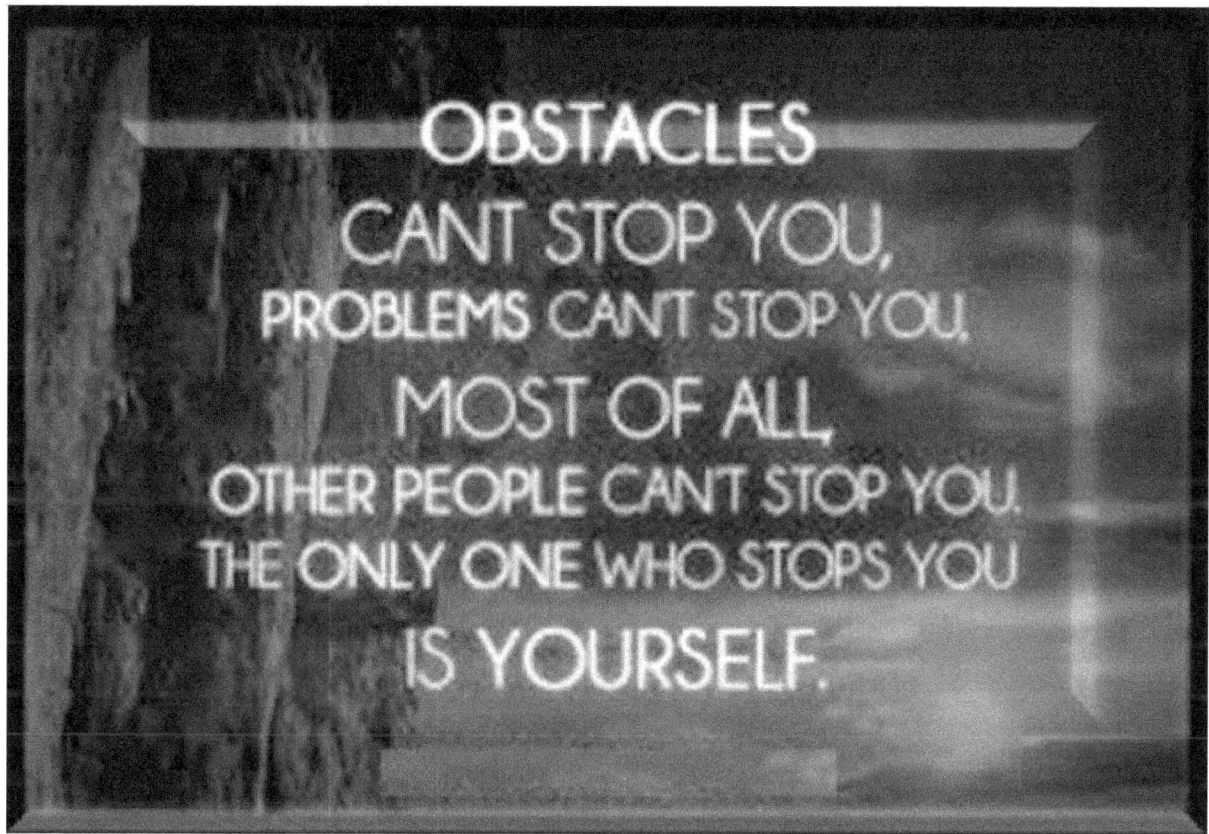

Self-determination is the formidable force that helps you to hold-on while pursuing a particular goal of life not minding the challenges that tends to keep you out of focus. It is the main instrument you use in conjunction with endurance, restraint and perseverance in the face of these challenges. Many go through the backdoor to achieve financial success because they lack patience and perseverance. My observation of people who achieved financial success in the past is that they embrace patience and perseverance. An important parts of these two all important ingredients for financial success is living within your means. In order word, living within your means is part of perseverance and patience. Spend less than you make and save money for the future and you can achieve financial independence. It is that simple. Even a little bit of savings will accumulate and grow into significant savings over the long term. It is the trend over the long term that makes the difference. Don't live a life of shadow; rather let your lifestyle reflect your financial status or size at that moment. It is no wisdom when you know you cannot afford a two bedroom apartment, but just because you have a friend living in a three bedroom; you went and hire a three bedroom apartment to let your friend know that you are in the same class. Agreed, you have elevated your housing status to three bedroom; when it comes to making payment for the house after your rent expires will you call your friend to assist you in offsetting the rent? Wisdom is the stability of your times. Instead, persevere and be patient. It is a matter of time you will get there. So don't eat your tomorrow today. Be wise.

Spreading your Financial Tentacles

In all human affairs there are efforts, and there are results, and the strength of the effort is the measure of the results obtained. If you have already built up a strong financial base for yourself, it is time to replicate and spread that success. Any success achieve and not improved upon continually will become outdate in no distant future. Gifts, power, material, intellectual capability, and spiritual possessions are the fruits of efforts; they are steps taken, thoughts completed, or vision realized. What are the things to do in order to replicate your financial success?

Continuous Improvement Lifestyle

Continuous improvement effort rather than strength of intelligence; is the key you need to spread out your financial tentacles. Financial success may be likened to a garden which is intelligently cultivated and monitored to prevent weeds from choking the plant. A land that is left alone, whether cultivated or neglected, must and will bring forth. If no useful seeds are continuously sown on it, an abundance of useless weeds will produce their kinds and make the farm grow wild. Just as a farmer continue to cut the weeds in his farm from time to time to allow desired plants to get enough nutrients for growth and survival, so must we continue to strive for a new level of financial success and better life. What we achieve today was as a result of the effort of yesterday; the effort of today will make way for the success of tomorrow. Not to cultivate any effort in the direction of our financial goal today is to expect nothing tomorrow.

To keep yourself on the track of financial success continuously, you have to keep improving on the success of today. The motor industries will give a good analogy on continuous improvement. For instance, a vehicle manufacture by Ford motor company in the 1960s was very valuable at that time because it is the best effort around then. The same vehicle if reproduced and sold to the market today will receive much less patronage from buyers, if not none. Each year, motor manufacturers follow market trends and buyers desires to produce the next series. Human tastes are changing continuously, and so must the manufacturer respond to this taste in order to get for their products, good share of the market. In all human endeavors there are exertions, and the strength of the exertion is the measure of the result you should expect.

There was this classmate of mine when I was in secondary school. He was the only child of his parents then, and much care and attention was given to him so he could get the best out of life. Because the parents are anxious to see him grow to become a child of reference among his equals, they sought to know about his tomorrow today. They consulted an oracle priest who confirmed to them that their son will be king of his town in the near future. The parents rather than keep the information to themselves and continue to encourage the young lad on his way to success; chose to divulge the future success envisioned by the oracle priest to the boy.

As soon as the boy received the good news, he was totally relaxed from his studies. Before then, he was one of the very good students in class. But after he was told about his future success as a king, he picks the bragging option. He was always telling us his classmates, *"do you know whether I study or not I will be your king, and I will judge all of you as I want"*.   Readers; that time the king of our village were predominantly illiterates; and the two things required to be a king were just prudence and previous experiences of the individual in managing community matters. Friends, to cut the long story short; while we gained admission into the university, our future king colleague was a dropout. True to the oracle priest's prediction, it came to the time for a new king to be enthroned; and the kingmakers were looking for possible candidates in the family house of our classmate. His name was chosen among the many possible candidates for the throne. Guest what my reader? He was overwhelmingly selected at first based on popularity. But in the second stage of the process he was eliminated on the ground that he was an illiterate, and the kingmaker made it clear to him that gone were the days when popularity alone can earn a man the kingship. And that today, due to the enormous roles of kings in public functions, an educated individual should be selected. So he lost his chance because he chose not to have a vision and improve on himself. Whatever you achieve as success today if not improved upon will be outdated in the near future. Your financial success now is only good for today, and if not improved upon, will become obsolete in no distant future.

Follow your Passion

Follow your dream or passion; or you will spend the rest of your life working for someone who followed his. Passion is living uncomfortably on purpose. It is choosing to stay up late and wake up early for a course you believe in. It is choosing to forgo certain luxuries and sometimes even some necessities in order to accomplish a purpose. It is choosing to look foolish, even when you care for what others think. If you don't build your dream, someone will hire you to help build theirs. You've got to follow your passion. You've got to figure out what it is you love, and who you really are. The only courage anyone ever need is the courage to follow his/her own dreams. Purpose is the reason for you embarking on a journey, and passion is the fire that lights up your path all the way through. Follow your passion, be prepared to work hard and sacrifice; and above all, do not allow anyone to limit your dreams. Be buried totally doing something that matters to you.

It is not that passionate people don't enjoy sleeping – they do. It is just that once they're up, they get excited about the work ahead of them. Even if the particular project or tasks they will be working on may not excite them, their future aspirations and the passion they have for what they do drive them to get out of bed rather quickly. Passionate people are very energetic about that thing that matters to them, so they get up early to see that it is on course; you can't do much if you spend half the day sleeping. Passion is buried into three basic human physical attributes for business success: Dedication, hard work and constant devotion to the course you believe in.

A) DEDICATION

Another name for dedication is commitment. It is the lubricating oil that greases your effort to succeed. It is to be excited about what you are doing. You cannot adjust your life around something if you do not care for it; love is what drives your motivation and allow you to invest your time and effort around that thing you love. If that sense of personal commitment is not there then there is no motivation. Therefore, it is motivation that keeps one from quitting any challenge of life. If the motivation is there, you will sacrifice your time; so we could also say that dedication is time, a whole ton of time in fact. You don't just become dedicated to something without your time involved. You become dedicated to it because of the amount of time spend on it. One wouldn't be considered dedicated to something if they spent just an hour a day on it; time and dedication go hand in hand. Be responsible and loyal to the course of action you belief in. Your body and mind must be up to full potential to accomplish the things you want to do when you are dedicated. You are dedicated to your course of action in life if you find yourself showing the following attributes:

- Put all your heart into achieving success in your course of action.
- Undiluted passion to pursue your course of action to a logical conclusion.
- Never give up at any time in the pursuance of your course of action.
- Be responsible to its outcome every step of the way.

B) HARD WORK

Hard work is the platform on which you can achieve everything valuable in life. If work is applying your ability, then hard work is applying your ability with focus and intensity to the exclusion of other possibilities. Some define hard work as anything you do that challenges you. And why is challenge important here? Why not just do what's easiest? Most people will do what's easiest and avoid hard work; and that is precisely why you should do the opposite. The superficial opportunities of life will be attacked by multitudes of people seeking what's easy. The much tougher challenges will usually see a lot less competition and a lot more opportunity. There is an African gold mine two miles deep. It cost tens of millions of dollars to construct, but it's one of the most lucrative gold mines ever. These miners tackled a very challenging problem with a lot of hard work, but ultimately it's paying off.

Strong challenge is commonly connected with strong results. Sure you can get lucky every once in a while and find an easy path to success. But will you be able to maintain that success, or it is just a coincidence? Will you be able to repeat it? Once other people learn how you did it, you will find yourself overloaded with competition. When you discipline yourself to do what is hard, you gain access to a realm of results that are denied everyone else. The willingness to do what is difficult is like having a key to a special private treasury room. The nice thing about hard work is that it is universal. It doesn't matter what industry you're in — hard work can be used to achieve positive long-term results notwithstanding the explicit.

I'm using this same hard work principle in building this personal development book. I put in a lot of valuable time possessions that are precious to me in getting things done; I put the writing of this book on top hierarchy on the scale of preference. I try to address topics that other people don't and bypass the low hanging fruit. I strive to explore topics deeply and search for the gold. I do lots of reading and research. I write lengthy articles and give my best ideas away for free, so I'm constantly forced to better my best. It's a lot of hard work. But I want this to be the kind of book that people will still be looking for ten years from now. Writing a book like this is at least ten times harder than the kinds of books I see dominating the psychology section of bookstores today. But most of those books will be off the shelves in a year, and few people will even remember them.

Definitely, hard work pays off. The greater your capacity for hard work, the more rewards fall within your grip. The deeper you can dig, the more treasure you can potentially find. Being healthy on its own is hard work. Finding and maintaining a successful relationship is hard work. Raising kids is hard work. Getting organized is hard work. Setting goals, making plans to achieve them, and staying on track is hard work. Even being happy is hard work (true happiness that comes from high self-esteem, not the fake kind that comes from denial and diversion).

Hard work goes hand-in-hand with acceptance. One of the things you must accept is that those areas of your life that won't succumb to anything less than hard work must be pursue with the mindset of acceptance. Perhaps you have had no luck finding a fulfilling relationship. Maybe the only way it's going to happen is if you accept you're going to have to do what you have been avoiding. It is time to accept that the path to your goal requires absolute discipline. Perhaps you want to increase your income. Maybe you should accept that the only way it will happen is with a lot of hard work. Your life will reach a whole new level when you stop avoiding and fearing hard work and simply surrender to it. Make it your ally instead of your enemy. It's a potent tool to have on your side. The following are signs that you currently embrace had work in your personal area of endeavor – be it in business or other goals of life:

- Survive the initial storm of starting a new business.
- You have reproduced yourself through your staff so as to expand your business.
- Establish a thriving business on dint of hard work.
- Bring in and teach your beneficiaries the rudiments of your business.

C) CONSTANT DEVOTION

Constant devotion to anything you belief in will propel you into achieving the success attached it. Action is the foundational key to all success in life. Your life does not get better by chance; it gets better by continuous improvement change you applied to it. Every day do something that will inch you closer to a better tomorrow. By changing nothing, nothing changes. Problems remain the way they are because people are busy defending rather than finding solutions to them; so stop wasting time defending that problem and work on addressing it instead. In the real sense of it, the secret of life is not in what happens to you, but what you do with what happens to you. The truth is that we all have abilities; but the results we get from our abilities vary widely because it depends on how we use it. The best preparation for tomorrow is to do today's work extremely well. The secret of getting ahead is getting started and giving a constant devotion to your course of action. If you don't go after what you want, you'll never have it. If you don't ask, you don't receive, and by not asking the answer is synonymous to not having what you want. If you don't step forward, you're always in the same place. The following attributes of personal constant devotion will help you achieve your goals:

- Nothing in the world can take the place of persistence.
- Have an addicted life–style to everything about what you belief in because it determines your future.
- If it is business, be a guru in it by studying every aspect of the business through continuous knowledge improvement – TRAINING/WORKSHOP attendance etc.
- Put in high degree of efforts commensurate with your future expectations always.
- Know that a journey of a thousand miles must begin with a single step; so ensure you are moving forward always.

- The world is not all sunshine and rainbows. It's a very mean and nasty place and I don't care how tough you are it will beat you to your knees and keep you there permanently if you let it.

Take Risks

Risk-taking is inseparable from financial success. In actual fact, everything about life is risk; whenever you engage in any action where the outcome is uncertain, you are taking a risk. You are taking a risk whenever you venture into the unknown, where your possibilities and probabilities cannot be determined to an exact degree. From the time you get up in the morning until you go to bed at night, and even when you are sleeping, you are taking a risk to some degree. It is how skillful and confident you are in taking the right risks for the right reasons to achieve goals that determines your success.

It is a known fact that every great leap forward in human life begins with risk-taking and a giant step of faith into the unknown. Men and women who achieve goals and accomplish wonderful things are invariably men and women of great faith in themselves and their abilities. The better you become at analyzing and assessing before taking a risk, and then avoiding as much of the risk as possible, the more competent and more capable you will become, and the more successful you will be.

Firms that gains competitive advantage from risk taking do not do so by accident. In the process of doing business, it is inevitable that you will be faced with unexpected and often unpleasant surprises that threaten to undercut and even destroy your business. That is the essence of risk and how you respond to it will determine whether you will survive and succeed. In fact, there are key elements that successful risk-taking organizations have in common. First, they succeed in aligning the interests of their decision makers (managers) with the owners of the business (shareholders) so that firms expose themselves to the right risks and for the right reasons. Second, they choose the right people for the task; some individuals respond to risk better than others. Finally, the culture of the organizations is conducive to sensible risk taking and it is structured accordingly. If there is a key to successful risk taking, it is to ensure that those who expose a business to risk or respond to risk; make their decisions with a common purpose in mind, and that is to increase the value of their businesses. If the interests of the decision makers are not aligned with those who own the business, it becomes inevitably clear that the business will be exposed to some risks that it should not have been exposed to.

Generally, in the world of investments and business; the importance of spreading one's risks is essential. No individual or company should be dependent upon one or two people for their financial well-being. One of the best ways to minimize risk-taking is to develop alternatives to what you are currently doing. The more alternatives you have, the lower your risk, and the higher the likelihood to achieve goals and reach your success in life. Having a number of alternative business or personal plans at your disposal therefore is a shock absorber in your pursuit of financial success.

The ability to achieve your set goals in financial success will be affected by the risk taking strategies you use in all areas of your life. You learn how to take intelligent risks without fear by taking a risk cleverly and then analyzing what happened. When you have clearly identified the risk involved, you can plan and prepare to maximize your opportunities while minimizing those risks. Your ability to confidently take calculated risks in the direction of your goals will ultimately help you achieve goals you set for yourself and lead you toward success in life.

Good risk takers have a combination of traits that seem mutually exclusive. They are realists who still manage to be optimistic; they tend to be realistic in their assessments of success and failure but they are also confident in their capacity to deal with the consequences. They allow for the possibility of losses but are not overwhelmed or scared by its prospects; in other words, they do not allow the possibility of losses to tilt their decision-making processes. They are able to keep both their perspective and see the big picture even as they are immersed in the details of a crisis; in terms of decision making, they frame decisions widely and focus in on those details that have large consequential outcome. Finally, they can make decisions with limited and often incomplete information; and make reasonable assumptions about the missing pieces.

Grow Beyond your Comfort Zones

In spreading out your financial success as an individual you must be willing to do without those things you cherish doing sometimes. One factor that helps people maintain positive self-regard is the feeling that they are growing and progressing in their lives. We all have a comfort zone: financial achievement, activities, places, people and routines that feel reassuring, predictable and comfortable. Comfort zones can be very beneficial, especially in times of stress and difficulty. However, it is possible to get "stuck" in our comfort zone in a way that limits possibilities for the kind of personal growth and development that can build self regard for us. Personal growth is multi-dimensional. It can include accomplishments and milestones in areas like learning, career, family and relationships, as well as emotional and spiritual growth. Personal growth can help individuals achieve what some writers have called self-actualization: a process of growth that helps people reach their full potential. If we don't seek out and act upon opportunities to develop to our full potential we may use only a small fraction of our true capabilities. Achieving our full potential requires that we move out of our comfort zones. It is a sacrifice for the financial future we want. Passion-driven individual grows beyond their comfort zones. It is being afraid and anxious, but taking positive steps in the direction of self-actualization. Fortunately there is a strong impulse to grow in every person, we all have ideas of what we wish to become.

We've heard it before; "move out of your comfort zone" is the familiar phrase spoken by many entrepreneurs, gurus and mentors. Moving out of a comfort zone requires us to break free from the past and push ourselves to do something we wouldn't ordinarily do. Some people believe in taking fairly radical steps. In the world of business, for example, experts commonly advise people to "do the thing you fear most." Facing fears successfully can give people a renewed sense of courage and a feeling that anything is possible. However this bold, fear-based approach is not for everyone. Sometimes, the simple act of trying a new activity can help people move beyond their comfort zones. For instance, cultivating the habit of saving if you don't do that before can be seen as taking positive steps out of your comfort zone. Denying yourself of the comfort of the moment in order to achieve a meaningful financial future is a step worth taking. Nothing beats having a bank account that you can turn to when life gets a bit hard. Making sure that you always have money stored away will definitely give you some peace of mind. Start by simply trying to follow your budget. Once you can do this then the next step is to be able to save money. Saving money requires you say no to yourself when you have the urge to spend it.

Here are 5 tips to help business owners' step outside their comfort zone and into the adventure and success zone:

1. **Change your Thoughts** – Everyone struggles with limiting thought patterns from time to time, but because thoughts drive feelings and behavior, it is important to learn to harness those negative thoughts and replace them with more reality-based, positive thoughts. It is absolutely true that when we choose to pay attention to the positive aspects of life this thought pattern orients our mind-body system toward success-inviting behaviors. Start by examining those pesky little "what if" questions that creep into our minds. Questions like, "What if I invest in this form of advertising and it doesn't work?", "What if I

open up my own office and can't get enough business to pay the rent?" These are the kind of fear-based questions that will keep you in your comfort zone. Harness those questions and replace them with positive "what if" questions. "What if I write some articles about my area of expertise and find I really enjoy it?" "What if I speak at an association meeting and was able to communicate my passion about my work?"

2. **Move through Fear with Action** – Use your fears to challenge yourself to new heights. The best antidote to fear is taking action. Take an adventurous approach to anything you fear. Are you afraid of calling that successful entrepreneur who might be able to help you out? Just do it – jot down a quick script, practice saying it out loud and then pick up that phone and call. Are you afraid to speak in front of groups? Perhaps you could join Toast Masters and learn how to speak in a group where everyone else is also learning. The crazy thing about fear is that it is an emotion that is rarely based on truth. Don't let some distorted version of reality stop you from making gains, start taking actions and move through the fear.

3. **Engage Your Mind** – Picture yourself reaching that next level of success. The brain can more easily create new neural pathways when we engage as many of the senses as possible, so create a mental movie that is rich in details. What would it look like when you reach that major goal? What kinds of sights, smells, tastes and feelings will you experience once you reach that goal? Take a few 5 minute breaks throughout the day to relax with deep

breaths and run your mental movie. The more you picture yourself accomplishing your goal, the more likely you are to move out of your comfort zone to create the new thoughts and behaviors needed to succeed.

4. **Participate in Hobby or Sport** – Take up a hobby or sport that moves you out of your comfort zone. Some entrepreneurs go sky-diving or wind-surfing – this allows them to experience the mind-body feeling state of doing something new and conquering fear. You do not necessarily need to take up a high-risk hobby or sport to move out of your comfort zone. You could try something as simple as hiking a little longer or higher than usual, taking a sculpting class, painting a picture without being concerned with the outcome or joining a community softball team. The emotional and mental experience of trying a new hobby or sport will translate to an expanded vision for your business. It will make it easier to try new approaches, think new thoughts, and attempt new ways of doing business.

5. **Consider Investing Money in Your Business** – When times are tight, our knee-jerk reaction is to tend to cut back on our marketing budget, research and development and new equipment or software. Instead of giving in to the temptation to slash growth-producing spending, find some confidence ways to invest in your business that will signal your own psyche that you are willing to put your money where your mouth is. This moves us out of our comfort zone by growing our faith in ourselves and in our business as well as putting some skin in the game.

Do Something Extraordinary

What is referred to as extraordinary is just a bit of extra beyond the ordinary that class you out of the many. If you must make your mark in the world of today, you must be willing to do beyond what your competitors are doing. Some people seem to get ahead, no matter what. They aren't necessarily smarter, more creative or harder working than many others. Still, they achieve much more than their peers. Why is that? The philosopher Aristotle offered an explanation a really, really long time ago: "We are what we repeatedly do. *Excellence is not an act, but a habit.*" They're amazing entrepreneurs, leaders, artists and innovators, and their keys to success aren't complex. Rather, it's the cumulative effect of their simple daily habits. People are doing extraordinary things in their businesses all the time. And there's no reason you can't be one of them. Just think about what could happen if you choose to make that difference hundred times every day for the next one year... You would have hundreds of thousands of small opportunities to make an impact. Now imagine if you do that for the next thirty years... You could change over a million outcomes for the better. That would be extraordinary.

We're all raised on the idea that we can be anything when we "grow up", and maybe it's just me, but I've always believed I have a bigger purpose. Being famous and writing books – my dream, as if there was no other option. It has always just seemed like fate. A path I was bound to follow. And as I've grown up, that hasn't seemed to change or fade. I still say "When I'm famous" not "If I'm famous". And maybe that's just me, with this fixed idea of fame and luck, or maybe that feeling of having a huge thing to do with my life. Like you are going to change the world; and there is nothing that can stop you.

The Five Personality Traits

Entrepreneurs come in all shapes and sizes, but the successful ones usually have a few things in common. There are five personality traits that point to entrepreneurial success. These personality traits have being tested overtime and are found to be the bedrock for business success.

1. **Vision** – While entrepreneurs need to be deeply enmeshed in the here and now of their current ventures, they also need a sense of the bigger picture. Successful entrepreneurs are always thinking ahead, planning the future with equal measures of imagination and wisdom.

2. **A Fighter's Instinct** – Like a seasoned boxer, a successful entrepreneur knows that winning takes more than a few swift punches. Both in the boxing ring and in business, the best fighters, study their competition to identify opponents' strengths and weaknesses, and then use that knowledge to develop a strategy to beat them. "When things are going well, the entrepreneur who thinks the fight is over and he has won will quickly find himself knocked to the mat," "Equally important is having the mental fortitude to keep fighting when you're at the bottom, bruised and bloodied."

3. **Passion** – The next personality trait is passion. The great thing about this intrinsic quality is that everyone has the capacity to develop it. So what is passion, really? "It's the source of incredible energy that feeds on one of our most powerful emotions and propels entrepreneurs forward with excitement and enthusiasm,"

4. **Confidence** – Any natural entrepreneur will burst with confidence, both in him or herself and in the conditions they control. Entrepreneurs need risk to thrive, so believing in themselves and the people they've put in positions of responsibility is essential. There's no room for doubt and

second-guessing yourself. I recommend that aspiring entrepreneurs should learn their own strengths and put them to good use; likewise you should know your own weaknesses. As an entrepreneur, you need to hire the right people to handle the jobs that don't play to your strengths. And this is just as important as fulfilling whatever role you choose for yourself.

5. **Change Agent** – What you visualize will materialize. I clearly believe that entrepreneurs can create their own realities. So if you're a conformist, you might consider another career path. Entrepreneurs need to be agents of change. You can't be content with maintaining the status quo; you must push the limits. Dare to be different!

Incorporate Good Financial Management

You may be wondering what exactly is meant by the term "financial management?" Financial Management is the process of managing the financial resources, including accounting and financial reporting, budgeting, collecting accounts receivable, risk management, and insurance for a business. It is the process you use to put your numbers to work to make your business more successful. With a good financial management system, you will know not only how your business is doing financially, but why. And you will be able to use it to make decisions to improve the operation of your business. Financial management of your small business encompasses more than keeping an accurate set of books and balancing your business checking account. You must manage your finances so you don't overspend and so you remain prepared for all expenditures, as well as profit distributions. Your financial management responsibilities affect all aspects of your business. A company that sells well but has poor financial management can fail.

Why is financial management important? Good financial management system enables you to accomplish important big picture and daily financial objectives for your business. A good financial management system helps you become a better macro-manager by enabling you to:

1. Manage proactively rather than reactively.
2. Borrow money more easily; not only can you plan ahead for financing needs, but sharing your budget with your banker will help in the loan approval process.
3. Provide financial planning information for investors.
4. Make your operation more profitable and efficient.
5. Access a great decision-making tool for key financial considerations.

Standard financial planning and control practice will also help you become a better micro-manager by enabling you to:

1. Avoid investing too much money in fixed assets.
2. Maintain short-term working capital needs to support accounts receivable and inventory more efficiently.
3. Set sales goals; you need to be growth-oriented, not just an "order taker."

4. Improve gross profit margin by pricing your services more effectively or by reducing supplier prices, direct labor, etc., that affect cost of goods sold.

5. Operate your business more efficiently by keeping the selling and general and administrative expenses down more effectively.

6. Perform tax planning.

7. Plan ahead for employee benefits.

8. Perform sensitivity analysis with the different financial variables involved.

In setting up a financial management system your first decision is whether you will manage your financial records yourself or whether you will have someone else do it for you. There are a number of alternative ways you can handle this. You can manage everything yourself; hire an employee who manages it for you; keep your records in-house, but have an accountant prepare specialized reporting such as tax returns; or have an external bookkeeping service that manages financial transactions and an accountant that handles formal reporting functions. Some accounting firms also handle bookkeeping functions. Software packages are also available for handling bookkeeping and accounting. The first step in developing a viable financial management system is the creation of financial statements. To manage proactively, you should plan to generate financial statements on a monthly basis. Your financial statements should include an income statement, a balance sheet and a cash flow statement. A good automated accounting software package will create the monthly financial statements for you. If your bookkeeping system is manual, you still can use an internal or external bookkeeper to provide you with monthly financial statements.

On the other hand, I have discovered that some people aren't meant for business ownership. Instead of increasing their income, they should strive to get better at their job and to climb the corporate ladder. Being a business owner requires discipline, responsibility and the ability to handle uncertainty. Some people can't handle being their own boss. For them, they need someone else telling them what to do or otherwise they will get nothing done. They also can't stomach the uncertainty of the ups and downs of being your own business owner. Get a job with steady income and you get to leave the office at quitting time and not have to worry about it until the next day. The buck stops with the business owner and they do have to worry at night if there is a huge problem in the business. Many have said, "*Job stands for Just Over Broke*". That may be true, but I would argue that some people who start their own business end up even more broke than if they would have stayed in their job.

5

Training and Education in Business Growth

Training of employees is essentially important to any organization because it determines whether the company achieves its corporate objectives (vision/mission). Perhaps its most positive beneficial effect is highly skilled employees. Investment in training has direct impact on the overall efficiency of any company, its growth index and the quality of employee the company has. Often, good training is just as important as good benefits package for all employees.

For employers, training allows them to locate a wider range of people with the kind of outlook that matches the company mission statement. The right kind of perspective is a hard thing to cultivate, whereas workplace specific proficiencies are easier to get. The other advantage employers should remember about training is that it offers them an improved employee retention rate. Employees are more loyal to companies that value their growth and want to cultivate it, and therefore provide a better performance and decrease the rollover rate at any company, no matter how small or large. If an employee thinks a company values him or her, that sentiment will go into whatever the employee is designing, selling, manufacturing etc; for the company. On the other hand, the kind of training an employee receives is very important. Allowing an employee to simply pass through a sort of substandard "101" training course does not ensure improvement. Every single part of the management in a company must completely sustain the training. Otherwise, there is no point in wasting even a substandard effort at training. Cheap training will result in cheap work: quality employees require quality training programs, which means spending a bit more. Excellent training programs emphasize a correlation between personal development and official evaluations, allowing an employee to discern that career growth and success means improving their expertise with training.

Impact of Training to Organizational Growth

The impact of training to organizations cannot be over emphasized. Training is of growing importance to companies seeking to gain advantage over competitors. A company with vision for growth in the future will play active role in the development of the potentials of all its employees. Part of the way a company encourages continuous staff improvement is through training. Improving employee skills is not only about improving skills related to their specific field, but also improving skills related to interpersonal and communication interactions. These abilities are constantly developing and perhaps more important than field related abilities. A person can be average in their field skills, but an excellent communicator with fantastic people skills is an asset to a company. These kinds of employees tend to fit better with a company. Other skills that should be emphasized besides those related to industry and interpersonal use; include how to manage time effectively, how to deal with disputes, and how to build a strong team.

How do you begin to create a business training program appropriate to your company? Detailed analysis on current employees is a good place to start asking what works and what does not. Ask them what kinds of things would help them improve because the right kinds of questions provide a company with a great return. Employees will improve job performance dramatically and the company overall success too.

There are many different types of skills that you use in running your business. Two most important skills for making your business successful are: Technical Skills and Business Management Skills.

Technical Skills: These are skills used to complete technical tasks or steps that are the basis of your business. For example, you may be able to build a website, host it and get it running on a server.

Business Management Skills: These skills are used in executing many tasks needed in operating a business, such as calculating profit, keeping records, and marketing goods or services to your customers.

If training is accounted for as cost rather than investment, then it is not valued by managers. If factors like employee engagement, customer retention and attainable increase in profits are important, then training will be a key driver. If cost management is the key focus, then training will take a back seat, and customer retention will be the medium term effect. Any organization that is looking to grow needs to balance two factors: Develop the Business, and Develop the People.

Many entrepreneurs are technical experts in what they do but start a business without any formal training or experience in management practices and principles. By "management" here I mean the business of successfully managing the non-technical side of the business, the "back room" activities. As a result of inadequate management, many small businesses fail in the early years. This is particularly common in many African countries, where more than sixty percent of businesses in their first generation never survive to the second. When the original owner passes on, the business dies within the space of one to three years. They fail not because of a weakness in the product or service concept they have, but because the business was not properly managed in the back office.

When the right tools, training and experience is coupled with good attitude, business success is guaranteed.

(Tool+Training+Experience) x Attitude = Goal/Success

Entrepreneurs are simply those who understand that there is little difference between obstacle and opportunity and are able to turn both to their advantage. Four keys to successful small business management are: (1) Owners have developed habits and traits that are positive, committed, patient and persistent. (2) A living strategic business plan is in place. (3) An organizational structure has been developed that encourages people to be their best and helps them do so. (4) Operational support systems are used that track performance and relieve senior management of daily detail, yet supply them with critical data to manage the business.

Seek Financial Advice

Successful financial management lifestyle is an ongoing process. It is important to continually monitor your spending, savings, and investments and adjust your plan as necessary. On a motivating note, you don't have to be an expert in financial management to achieve financial success, but a good understanding of the basics will help you; and put you in control of your money.

Financial matters, while very much a part of our lives, can be complicated at times. If you feel a little lost in some areas of personal finance, call upon an expert for help. There is no shame in not knowing everything. After all if you're sick, you go to a doctor; if your car breaks down, you take it to a mechanic. Financial planners, investment advisors, credit counselors, and insurance agents are examples of the types of financial experts that you can get help from. You can also continue to learn on your own. An article on investments could be by a certified financial planner. There are a multitude of books and periodicals on personal finance, and many of them can be found at the library, so you don't even need to buy them. Dreamers are the savior of the world. The visible world is governed by the invisible; dream lofty dreams. And as you dream, so you will become. Your vision is the promise of what you will become one day. Your idea is the prophecy of what you shall at last unveil.

Finding the right financial advisor is the first step toward receiving good financial advice. To save both time and money, the most productive way you should go about this is to rely on those you trust to refer you to someone they either work with or know personally. Friends and family are your best options, but it's also a good idea to consult with your accountant or lawyer to steer you in the right direction, especially since most financial advisors work closely with professionals from any of these fields.

Interviewing at least four to five financial advisors from different firms will give you an unbiased opinion when deciding on whom to work with. Most advisors don't charge fees for initial meetings, so don't be shy when asking for a complimentary interview. Go to each meeting prepared with a list of questions. Your questions should address things such as how long advisors have been in business, the demographics of their current clients and the average net worth of each client.

The answers you receive will help you make your decision, so be selective with your questions. For example, if you find that the advisor's clients' average net worth is drastically different when compare to yours, you should question his or her ability or willingness to service you. In addition, an advisor who works primarily with retirement plans for small businesses may not be a good fit if you're looking for estate-planning advice. During the interview process, a good advisor will gather basic information about you and, in many cases, will address immediate concerns relevant to your situation. For example, if the advisor learns that you recently received a large lump-sum payment from a settlement or inheritance, he or she should emphasize the impact that taxes may have on your investments. This should give you the impression the advisor cares and knows how to help you.

Once you've narrowed your selection down to two or three advisors, expect each one to want to get to know you a bit more (i.e., what you do for a living, what you do for fun, who your spouse is, how many kids you have, etc.). Advisors should solicit as much information about you as they can, to develop a complete understanding of your financial situation. This includes your sources of income and savings, spending habits, life and medical insurance, inheritances and even things such as health issues and family history. All these factors play a significant role in a good financial advisor giving comprehensive recommendations. In most cases, financial advice is unique to each situation, so an advisor's analysis is important when recommending one product over another. Expect advisors to diagnose your financial situation before prescribing you advice. For example, a recommendation to establish a life insurance trust doesn't mean everyone with life insurance should own a trust. Or a recommendation to purchase a tax-free municipal bond doesn't mean you should be buying bonds. In both cases, you'll end up paying unnecessary commissions and/or fees.

The advisor's plan of action should address both your short- and long-term goals and how you are to go about accomplishing them. Also, it might make more sense to direct permanent life insurance premiums toward other savings vehicles for retirement, because the cost of the policy may not justify your intentions. Your strategy should allow you to adequately adapt to life-altering events, and it should change as life changes. Life may throw you unexpected dusts, so it's important you revisit your strategy on an ongoing basis. This should be done in regular, recurring meetings with your advisor on a quarterly, semi-annual or at least annual basis, depending on your needs.

Read Financial Success Books

A lot of people are looking for investment enlightenment on the Internet; can I say this clearly that you are looking at the wrong place. You are not going to find much of it on the web. I suggest you log off, power down your computer, and read some books. Take your time. The months you spend perusing this list will be well spent and I can assure you that you'll get value for your money. I happen to be an educationist in the area of finance, and by divine providence I have authored at least four books relating to growing, managing and investing your money. I'd recommend reading at least the four books listed below before even thinking of getting your hands dirty with developing, investing and managing your money. There is what to do in order to get the results you expect. You can find them cheaply in these books, all you need to do is to apply them as specified; and you'll see a sudden progressive change coming into your life that will establish your financial solvency.

1. **Financial Wisdom in the Days of Small Beginning** – This is one of my books that discussed how you can walk your way into financial success through the application of basic financial wisdom principles and practices. The central tenet of the book is that a scientific approach should be used when directing your investments. Great things have small beginnings. The benefit of small beginning is often lost on us when we face the possibility of embarking on a new dream. It takes financial wisdom to succeed in your finances. Financial wisdom is simply the ability to use your mind which is the greatest resource you have to attract some principles and values to your financial life. Your desire for

change must be so strong that it becomes the very breath of your life. It must be your first thought when you wake up and your last thought when you go to bed at night. It must be in the forefront of everything that you do! You will discover in this book, incredibly helpful personal finance wisdom that I wish someone would have told me a long time ago.

2. **Financial Worries? Try This!** – This book is also another of my books. It is a piece of writing on overcoming financial worries, and it is designed to assist you in building a strong financial future through tested principles and uncommon practices of many years of personal financial development effort. Financial uncertainties or worries occur in everyone's life. However, the degrees of worries everyone experience depends on your societal status or class. This book explains the fundamental steps to overcoming financial worries. Sometimes it seems as if everything happens all at once. Financial worries seem to pile up one on top of the other. If your business isn't going on as planned or envisioned, what is holding you back? You might probably say it is lack of capital, lack of employee, lack of time, so many family responsibilities and so on. But these reasons are not what caused your lack of financial success. These reasons are merely the results of a great cause – inability to respond to opportunities in time. Opportunities come as a flash and varnishes in no time. When dedication, hard work and constant devotion is mixed with opportunities, financial success is guaranteed.

3. **Financial Success Toolkit** – This book is one of my books on launch-pad series. This book contains financial success tools designed to assist you in building a strong financial future for yourself. It explains the details you need to follow in order to enjoy positive progressive change in your financial empowerment goals! If a man change the way he thinks, and apply himself to the course of positive actions and opportunities available to him; he will be surprise at the rapid transformation the effect of the change will bring to him; more often than not, in the comfort and material things of life. We often imagine that thought can be kept secret, but it cannot; rather it rapidly crystallizes into habits, and habits solidify into circumstances. Thoughts of fear, financial insecurity, doubt, and indecision crystallizes into weak, unmanly, and indecisive habits which solidify into circumstances of failure. On the other hand, a positive and determinate thought of all kinds crystallizes into habits of grace, temperance, courage, self determination and self control. The results of such thought is success, plenty, and freedom of all kind – including financial freedom!

4. **Millionaire Next Door** – This book covers much of the same ground as the books mentioned above with more emphasis on seven steps you should follow to succeed financially. The first rule is, always live well below your means. The last rule is, choose your occupation wisely. You'll have to buy the book to find out the other five. It's only fair. The authors' conclusions are commonsensical. But, as they point out, their prescription often flies in the face of what we think wealthy people should do. There

are no pop stars or athletes in this book, but plenty of wall-board manufacturers--particularly ones who take cheap, infrequent vacations! Stanley and Danko mercilessly show how wealth takes sacrifice, discipline, and hard work, qualities that are positively discouraged by our high-consumption society.

All these books can be found at eBay Kindle store. Many of today's most successful money managers obtained their original financial inspiration from these four books. It is always fun to look at excesses in the marketplace and ask, "What would Victor say about this?" This 2012 edition benefits from annotation by one of finance's most brilliant observers, Stanley Gonah.

Get Inspiration from Successful Business Owners

Entrepreneurship can be a lonely game. The road to business success, both online and offline, is a long and bumpy one, often littered with pitfalls before success comes knocking. You need to be willing to spend long hours learning and applying new information when you should rather be spending time having fun with family and friends. It can take several attempts and wrong turns before you hit on the right business model that not only works but also fits in with your life plan, vision and goals. The truth is, once you decide to leave the safety net of your day job to build your own business, you are stepping onto a crazy rollercoaster ride.

Amongst all the fun and excitement of being your own boss, there will be days when you feel scared, alone and confused. Deals you were banking on fall through. People you thought you could trust let you down. Products you thought would be home-runs flop embarrassingly. During tough times like these there isn't much you can do, other than keep the faith and keep going. I'm a passionate believer of the fact that being in business involves mastering the inner game of self and the outer game of business. Having a success mindset is essential, possibly even more important than business acumen alone. That's why I am such a fan of motivational and inspirational quotes. They keep me focused and positive, even when things are not going as planned.

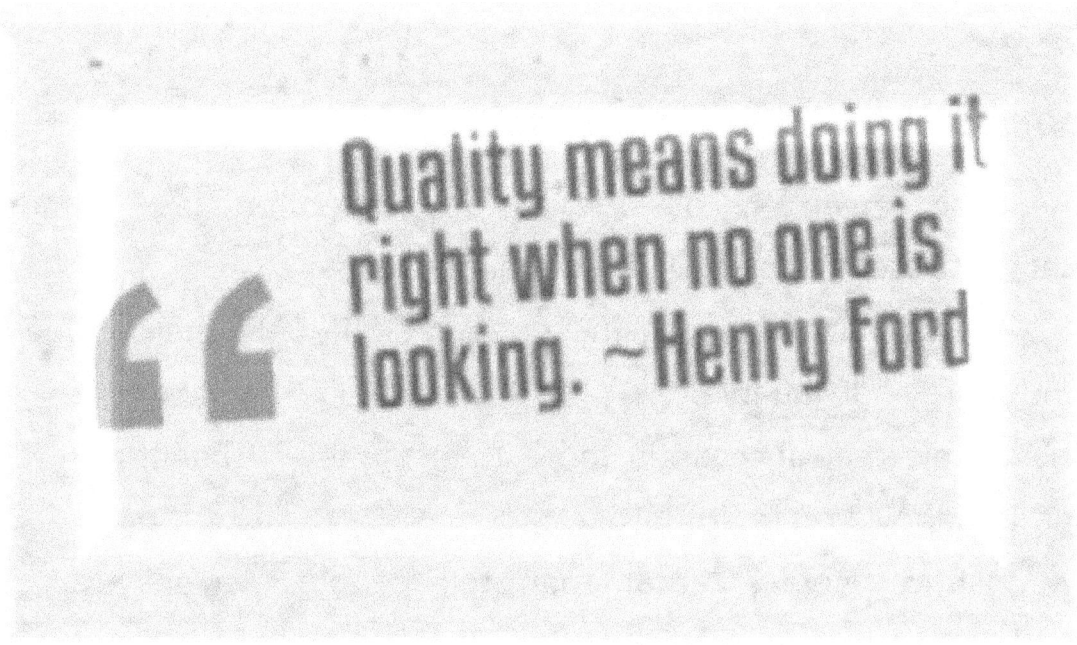

With this in mind I make bold to say that the best way to learn is to rely on the experiences of others who has journeyed the road you are planning to travel. To be truly successful in business you should draw from past experiences of successful business owners. They have a lot to share with you on making success of your own business. They have experienced the ups and down, and can give clues on how to take your steps on a slippery terrain of personal business adventure. So it is part of the training and education you need to succeed in that business. Over the years I have had relationships with thousands of business owners. Many of these were successful, some were massively successful. I noticed that the most successful business owners shared certain habits. They did things which the average business owner would not do. I decided to learn from them... to acquire their habits, to see if it would help me. It did. It really did; in big, meaningful, and measurable ways. So in brief, here is what I learned from them:

Important Habits for Business Success

1. They are driven by passion to do something big. Something that motivates them AND those around them.
2. They personalize their business, so it's uniquely theirs. One of a kind. Rare and valuable.
3. They know that success is more than money... that if you're rich and unhappy, you're still broke.
4. They show people, rather than tell people. Anyone can claim anything, so they walk the walk.
5. They out-care their competition. It shines through everything they do.
6. They out-smart their competitors too.
7. They set standards, extremely high, self-imposed standards... and they achieve them.
8. They ignore the manual and write their own rules.
9. They focus on what they want, not what they fear.

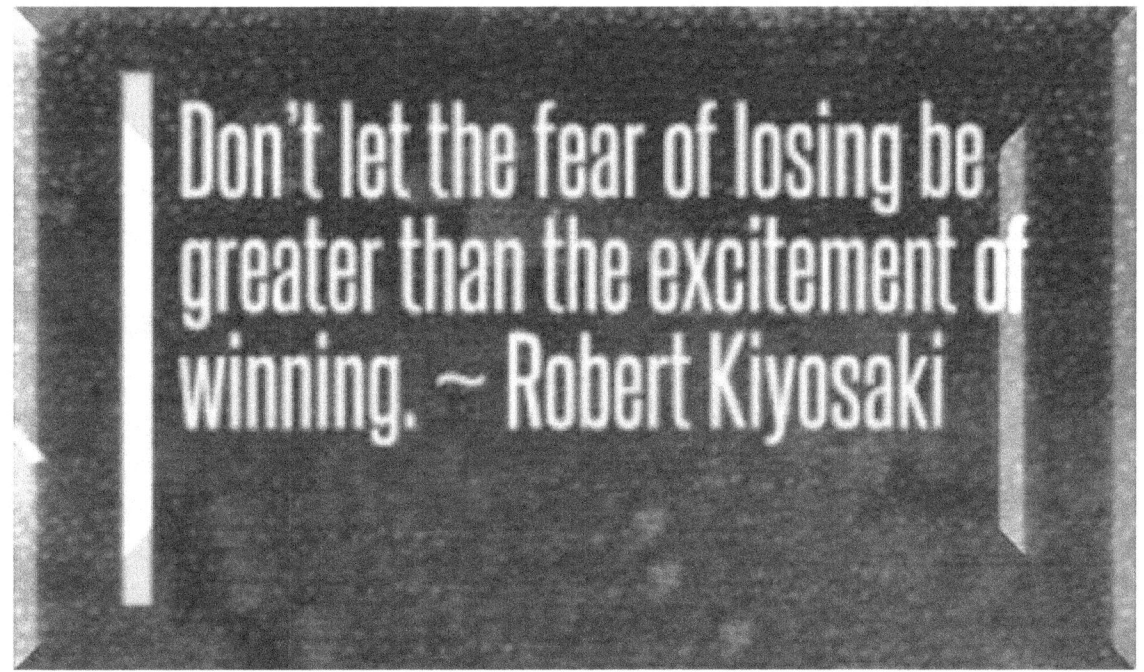

10. They are excellent decision-makers. They get the information required; study it, request advice if needed, then decide.

11. They avoid those costly diversions, which come disguised as shortcuts to success.

12. They work hard. You can't sleepwalk your way to the top... or even the middle.

13. They also relax. If you work smart during work time, you can relax when it's family and friends time.

14. They seldom watch TV. None of the most successful people I know, bother with TV.

15. They are extremely selective who they associate with and who they recommend.

16. They lead. The world already has enough followers and the followers need leaders.

17. They manage their time extremely well.

18. They deliberately build a valuable network of people — before they need them.

19. They are willing to stand out. They know it's the only way to be outstanding.

20. They summon the courage to do what's required, rather than what feels comfortable.

21. They make promises and ensure these promises are kept.

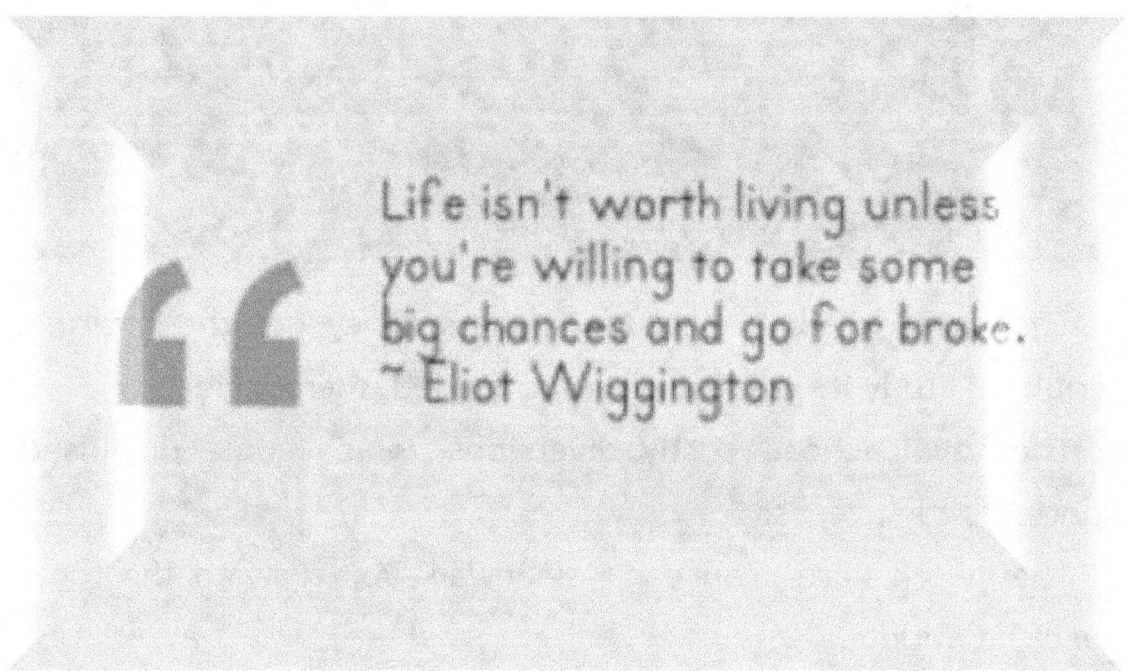

" Life isn't worth living unless you're willing to take some big chances and go for broke. ~ Eliot Wiggington

Think about your co-workers and clients. Are they inspiring you to do better in your business? Are they motivating you to try harder and move your business forward in a meaningful way? If not, then maybe it's time to reconsider the kind of people you work with. Co-workers who fail to inspire you are a liability. The same is true of average clients, with their average demands, average projects and average fees. Rather surround yourself with people who push you to create your best work. Without controversy, the impact this can have on your business is enormous. This will help you.

6

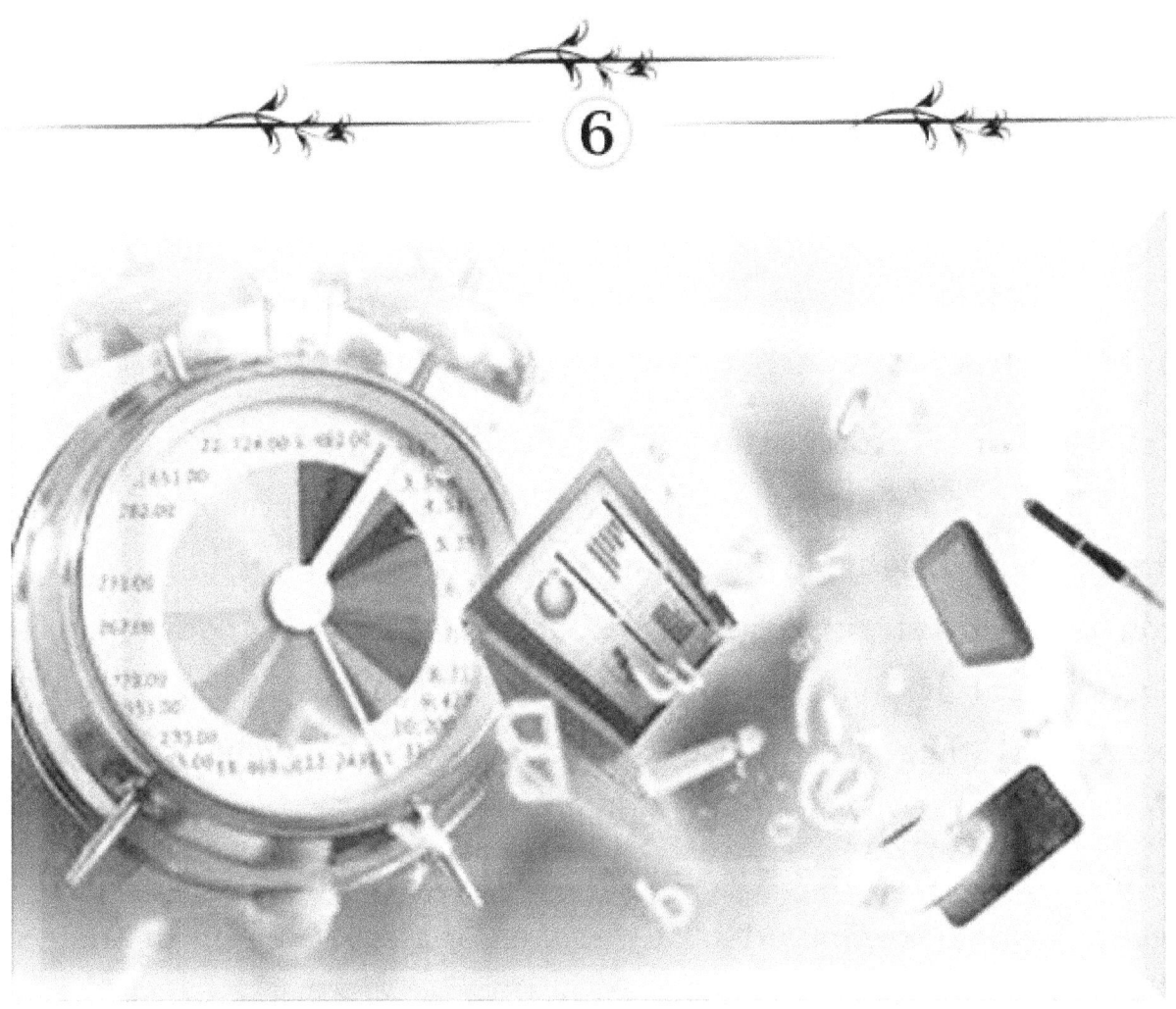

Time Management and Productivity

Finding a successful time management strategy depends on a person's personality, ability to self-motivate and level of self-discipline. Having enough time is a challenge for many small business owners. There just never seems to be enough time to get everything done, especially when you're wearing a lot of different hats and taking on many different roles in order to run your business. Not only is it frustrating, but it can be stressful to feel like you're bouncing from task to task and never really crossing things off your list. While we can't change the number of hours in a day, we can change the way we use them in order to manage time better and become more productive. It's not easy, and it can take a great deal of commitment and discipline, but it's possible to make time an ally of your business, not an enemy.

The Value of Your Time

Time is money, stop wasting it. Money is a standard universal means of exchange for goods and services. If time is money, this translates to the fact that time is an essential component of any human life. Once you've lost it you can never get it back. Studies show that employees spend about 31 hours per month in meetings, and spend less than 60 percent of time actually working productively. Having work for a university college right after graduating from the university, I came to understand the value of an hour very early on in my career. As a team leader, I know how important it was then to place value on the time of my colleagues. My time is worth more than my staff's, and their time is worth more than an intern's. Everyone understands this dynamic and plans accordingly. It helps us to decide whether a task is better left to an intern or if it should be better to manage up by regular staff. By determining the relative importance and time-sensitivity of tasks, it makes it much easier to assign and complete them in the most productive manner possible.

Assigning monetary value to both tasks and employees helps clear schedules of time-sucking activities that drag on production. An hour-long, 20-person meeting where only 10 people really need to be in attendance translates to more than a full workday's worth of wasted time. If we all treated our minutes a little more like dollars, there might be less time spent on Facebook and fantasy football and more spent moving our organizations forward. Friends your time is invaluable, and how you use it determines what you make out of life. Every human being have twenty four hours each day. What you do with your twenty four hours for twenty two days, determine what you get at the end of the month. Please value your time.

Managing Your Time for Productive Effort

You may never get everything done each day at your workplace; there will always be a few items leftover every day that you didn't get completed. The only time this is dangerous is when that leftover item is a high-priority item with a deadline attached. In order to avoid that from happening, take time to clarify what your priorities are and then schedule time to do your most important tasks when you are most productive. This is where personal goal setting meets time management. Goals cost time, which is finite. If you choose to be or have something, you choose to exclude something else, at least for now.

Time Management and Goal Setting

The foundation of good time management is to know where you're going and how to get there. Goals can help you create a plan to do just that. You put yourself in control, not others. You are an adult and you must make the transition from being told what to do by others to telling yourself in an intelligent way what to do. That is a skill that is not easy to acquire. The following are the importance of goal setting:

- Goals keep you motivated.
- Goals make you better at performance in all areas of life (personal, academic, career, etc.)
- Prevent you from being too hard on yourself.

Goal setting doesn't have to be reactive. The alternative is proactive or conscious personal goal setting; much less common, far more powerful. When you react, your 'goals' are, in essence, reflexes that do little more than scratch the latest itch. They send you off on a tangent that almost certainly doesn't align with your roles and values. Choose proactive goals and you'll match them to who you are and what you care about. Your values, roles, goals and actions are all in alignment. We all want to achieve our goals in life. Whether it's a possession, a position or a state of mind, everybody wants something. Within reason, anyone can achieve anything, as long as they're prepared to pay the price for it. Personal goal setting isn't hard once you have a clear idea how to set goals that contribute to your personal development. Do that and we will all benefit.

Schedule your Time and Set Priorities

If you control your time, you are indirectly controlling your life. Time is a precious commodity; everyone gets an equal share but we use it very differently. Most of us spend too much time on what is urgent and not enough time on what is important. Balance your effort. Listing your tasks is an important first step in prioritizing and time management.

Work on small portions every day of work that will be due by the end of the week, starting with the most important tasks first. Do today's tasks. Concentrate on what is at hand; do not allow yourself to lose focus. Then move on to the next daily task. Once today's tasks are completed, mark them as such, and proceed to tomorrow's tasks. When tomorrow's tasks are completed, work on the other tasks due by the end of the week, and when those are complete, work on the tasks due early next week. A small portion of each is better than one huge, laborious task and will keep your time managed more efficiently and reduce stress and eliminate burn-out. Make one of your final daily tasks the completion of tomorrow's task list. Close each day with a new task sheet for tomorrow to keep you on track.

Furthermore, focus on your most productive time of the day to do most of the tasks. One of the greatest time wasters is spending 95% of one's time on 5% of the tasks needed to be completed. This is the Pareto Principle; and the assumption is that the 5% seem to be the most profitable. This is not always true. Sometimes the five percent could take a lot of time, and may not give the expected result, but takes the chunk of the time. Don't allow work particularly less important ones to take longer than it should. If ten minutes is all a job is worth, make sure it's done in ten minutes. Take advantage of your profitable time. Some people work better in the morning, and some are more focused in the evening. Be at your best at your own time. Keep track of your progress. Cross out tasks off the list as they are completed. You'll feel more relieved and relaxed just by getting through the daily tasks. Not only will you be getting things done;

finishing the tasks will give you a sense of accomplishment and spur motivation.

Set realistic deadlines for all your tasks. With long-term projects, set interim deadlines and a final deadline. Allow time for contingencies; the longer the project, the more contingency time will be required. Decide whether your deadlines are fixed or flexible. Schedule your work to suit your personality at different times of the day or week. For example, if you're at your liveliest and most outgoing in the late morning, schedule your customer calls at that time.

Rewrite and prioritize your list on a regular basis. Add new tasks to the list. This should be done on a daily basis, especially when you are just getting started with a time management routine. Eliminate or adjust tasks that are completed, or fall in priority. Delegate tasks to others. Contrary to popular belief, you don't need to do it all. You can be much more effective if you can delegate tasks as necessary. Use technology to complete tasks more quickly, efficiently or accurately. Today's mobile technology gains parades dozens, if not hundreds of apps that will help you manage, and even accomplish your tasks efficiently.

Leave time for fun. While there are times when we just need to power through a large project, it's important to give yourself time to let loose. Not only will it refresh your mind, it's good for your body too. It doesn't have to be a lot of time but make sure that you do! Prioritized schedules must allow time for family. When you ignore family, everyone's unhappy.

Work on the Right Things

Maximizing the use of your time can be achieved by working on the right things. The key is not to prioritize what's on your schedule, but to schedule your priorities. Majority of people spend so much time on what is urgent and not enough time on what is important. Not all urgent tasks are significant. You cannot maximize your productivity if you don't even know where your time is running off to in the first place; and this time is spent mostly on the wrong things. So get down everything that is irrelevant or not serving your time well so you can manage your day better.

In addition to choosing the right things to do, the complete elimination of distractions is the only way to get neck-deep into your work, focused on the work and avoid fragmented sessions where you get nothing completed at the end. How much more could you achieve if you did the work you needed to do, the way you needed to do it, and eliminated the half-work, half-wandering that fill most of your day. If most important things are done first, there will be no day when you did not get something important done. By following this simple strategy, you will usually end up having a productive day, even if everything does not go as planned.

Some activities must be done at a specific time, e.g. an appointment to talk to an advisor. Other activities need to be done but can be done at any available time. Wisdom demand that those that must be done; should be done at that particular time. The goal of handling a task assigned to you is to make it better each time you work on it. This is referred to as work progression. Be time-conscious.

Give Account of Your Time

A management consultant by name Todd Herman defined personal accountability as "being willing to answer … for the outcomes resulting from your choices, behaviors, and actions." When you are personally accountable, you take ownership of situations that you are involved in. You see them through, and you take responsibility for what happens – good or bad. You don't blame others if things go wrong. Instead, you do your best to make things right. Giving account of your time is an effective way of improving your time management skill. Have you ever tracked your time, to see how you spent it? Have you ever really counted the minutes you spent working, playing, eating, sleeping and socializing on any given day? You might be genuinely surprised by the numbers. I know I was. This involves logging your activities in some detail over a given period, for instance a week.

Recently there was a week where I had fallen behind on my writing goal. There was just simply not enough time! Life got busy, it happens sometimes. I had a lot of stuff going on. I had a number of hours in my head that I felt like I needed to be writing every week. It was eight. That might sound kind of low for a promising writer like myself, but hey, I've got a full time job, performances and practices and I've also got a time of meditation to maintain. I had to be realistic, you know?

After that day I decided to start tracking my time. I spent a full week looking at how much time I spent writing, meditating, attending functions, or at my regular work place; versus how much time I consumed on all forms of media – movies, television, video games, podcasts, and even the internet). From my discovery, the time spent on all media was huge; and I was determined to make a change immediately. In the workplace, accountability can go beyond your own tasks. For example, you may be held accountable for the actions of your team.

⑦

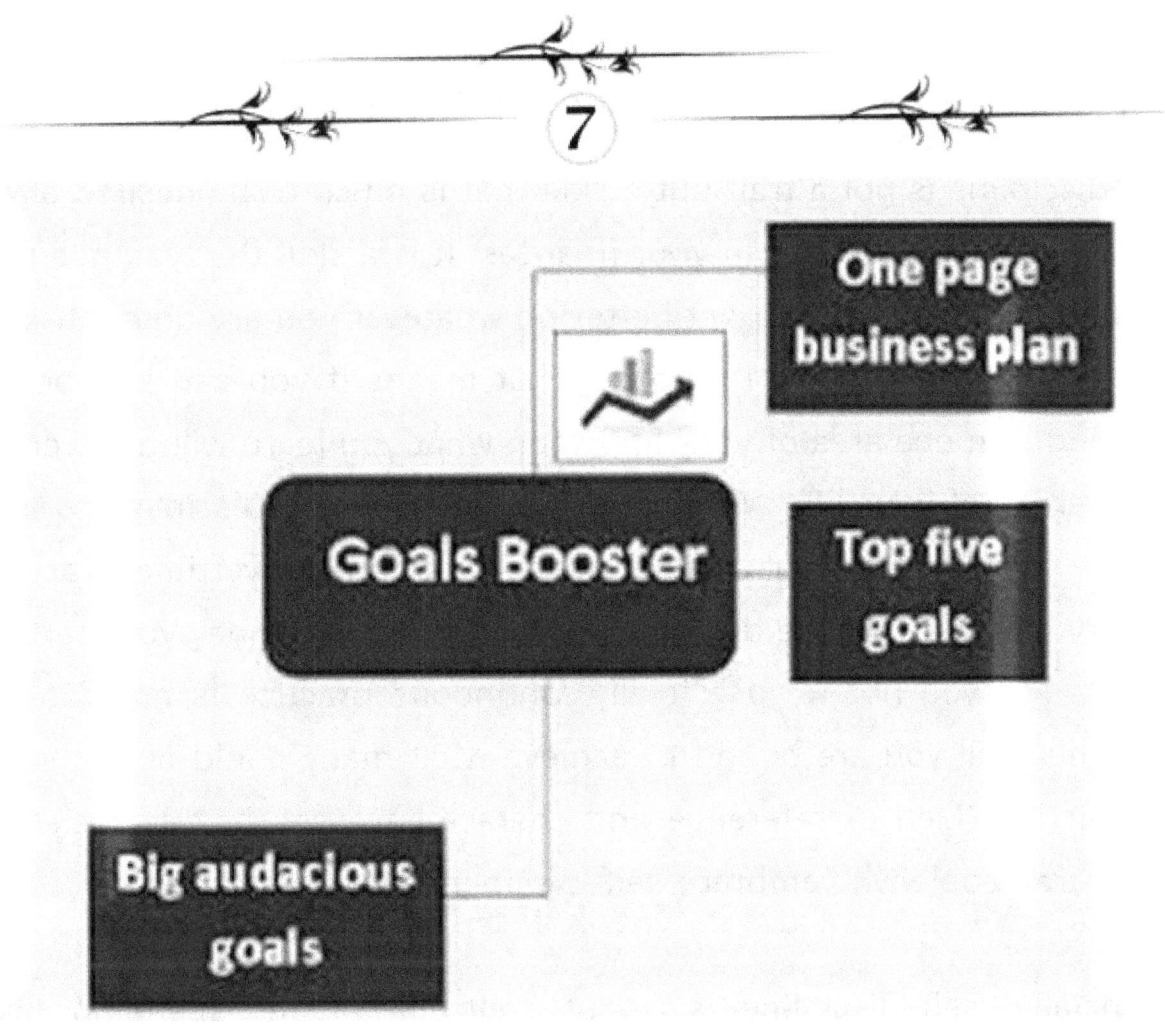

Goal Boosters on your Way

Imagine you set a goal to break the world record for badminton. You would want to be prepared, right? You would train hard. You would eat right. You would avoid any bad decisions. You would not try the high jump while wearing a bag full of rocks and heavy things, would you? A bad life decision can be like a heavy weight that holds you down. But good life decisions and good habits can do the opposite—they can boost you to success.

Self-Discipline a Vital Skill in the Pursuit of Success

Self-discipline is not a trait but a skill that is much to be desired after if you choose to succeed in your finances. It is a skill that you need to constantly use in order to get better on whatever you are doing. It is a skill that gets better with practice. That means if you can just begin applying it in one area of your life, soon what you learn will transfer to other areas of your life. When you are able to apply discipline to any area of your life the results will dramatically improve overtime. Practice it every day. Because the day you stop practicing is the day you start to lose it. For you not to lose it all, continuous practice is mandatory. With this skill you are bound to achieve what many could not achieve in their life. Men of reference and character we see in our societies today are people who embrace self-discipline with open arms.

Financially, self-discipline is about controlling your spending and making sure you pay for the things that need to be paid for. The hardest part for most people is controlling their spending. If you cannot control your spending then no matter how much money you make it will never be enough. Your wants will always use up whatever income you acquire. Thus, controlling what is spent is a necessity for everyone. It is being able to say NO to purchases you normally make on an impulse. These impulse purchases are the primary contributors to people not following their budget. You can make a budgetary amount to account for impulse purchases but then make sure you do not go over that amount on a monthly basis.

Those who do not have an iota of self-discipline must acquire it the hard way. Acquiring it comes from learning to practice it in small amounts. Start by simply trying to follow your budget. Once you can do this then the next step is to be able to save money. Saving money requires you say NO to yourself when you have the urge to spend money. We often think we "must" when in truth there is no urgency for it.

Risk-Taking and Financial Success

It is a known fact that every great leap forward in human life begins with risk-taking and a giant step of faith into the unknown. Men and women who achieve goals and accomplish wonderful things are invariably men and women of great faith in themselves and their abilities. The better you become at analyzing and assessing before taking a risk, and then avoiding as much of the risk as possible, the more competent and more capable you will become, and the more successful you will be.

Risk-taking is inseparable from financial success. In actual fact, everything about life is risk; whenever you engage in any action where the outcome is uncertain, you are taking a risk. You are taking a risk whenever you venture into the unknown, where your possibilities and probabilities cannot be determined to an exact degree. From the time you get up in the morning until you go to bed at night, and even when you are sleeping, you are taking a risk to some degree. It is how skillful and confident you are in taking the right risks for the right reasons to achieve goals that determines your success.

In the same way, firms that gains competitive advantage from risk taking do not do so by accident. In the process of doing business, it is inevitable that you will be faced with unexpected and often unpleasant surprises that threaten to undercut and even destroy your business. That is the essence of risk and how you respond to it will determine whether you survive and succeed. In fact, there are key elements that successful risk-taking organizations have in common. First, they succeed in aligning the interests of their decision makers (managers) with the owners of the business (shareholders) so that firms expose themselves to the right risks and for the right reasons. Second, they choose the right people for the task; some individuals respond to risk better than others. Finally, the culture of the organizations is conducive to sensible risk taking and it is structured accordingly. If there is a key to successful risk taking, it is to ensure that those who expose a business to risk or respond to risk; make their decisions with a common purpose in mind, and that is to increase the value of their businesses. If the interests of the decision makers are not aligned with those who own the business, it becomes inevitably clear that the business will be exposed to some risks that it should not have been exposed to.

Generally, in the world of investments and business; the importance of spreading one's risks is essential. No individual or company should be dependent upon one or two people for their financial well-being. One of the best ways to minimize risk-taking is to develop alternatives to what you are currently doing. The more alternatives you have, the lower your risk, and the higher the likelihood to achieve goals and reach your success in life. Having a number of alternative business or personal plans at your disposal therefore is a shock absorber in your pursuit of financial success.

The ability to achieve your set goals in financial success will be affected by the risk taking strategies you use in all areas of your life. You learn how to take intelligent risks without fear by taking a risk cleverly and then analyzing what happened. When you have clearly identified the risk involved, you can plan and prepare to maximize your opportunities while minimizing those risks. Your ability to confidently take calculated risks in the direction of your goals will ultimately help you achieve goals you set for yourself and lead you toward success in life.

Good risk takers have a combination of traits that seem mutually exclusive. They are realists who still manage to be optimistic; they tend to be realistic in their assessments of success and failure but they are also confident in their capacity to deal with the consequences. They allow for the possibility of losses but are not overwhelmed or scared by its prospects; in other words, they do not allow the possibility of losses to tilt their decision-making processes. They are able to keep both their perspective and see the big picture even as they are immersed in the details of a crisis; in terms of decision making, they frame decisions widely and focus in on those details that have large consequences. Finally, they can make decisions with limited and often incomplete information; and make reasonable assumptions about the missing pieces.

Live Your Size Per Time

Friends, don't live a life of shadow; rather let your lifestyle reflect your financial status or size at that moment. The key to financial success or financial independence is living within your means. It's great to pursue our dreams and have the life we want. But try to put a demarcation between your need and want. Your need are what is necessary and compulsory you must buy while wants are those things you desire but not so essential. Best thing to do is to first take care of what you need, and then consider what you don't need but really want later if you have budget surplus. In the immediate past paragraph I did mention about setting up a budget. When a budget is in place it guides your spending, and you are able to live within what you plan to spend over that period of time. Be mindful to eliminate your excesses.

You know what you earn, so let your income guide you on what kind of lifestyle you should live. For instance your salary dictates that your spending should be among the middle class; but rather than keep to it, you are copying a friend whose spending is among the top class. For sure, you will soon be in financial tight corner shortly. What might be a simple, no-worry for many people might be incredibly challenging for others due to their current financial circumstances. So be guided by your spending lifestyle. Some people just let emotions get the best part of them when shopping. Having self-discipline can be a great initiative not only for finances, but for other aspects of life as well. Good judgment can be a great antidote for excess emotion when shopping, and an essential part of financial success. You need conscious effort in order to embrace a modest lifestyle. It is the deliberate application of your willpower and strength of mind to overcome the situations that come your way in the actualization of your life goals. It is certain that every ambition in life has challenges attached to it. Your resolve to overcome these challenges is what gives you the breakthrough you desire.

Avoid Procrastination

The proverb *'procrastination is the thief of time'* should ring a bell in anyone's ears. Time is an essential aspect of life for every human being. Time once lost, is lost forever. Usually, our time for a particular thing elapses if we are either late or we postpone doing it. The more we delay or procrastinate, the more we tend to lose out on many things of life. After all, time is money. Time is treasure that is inexplicable – a mystery we must set out to find out. By procrastinating, we are rescheduling the things in our lives that shouldn't necessarily be overlooked. Putting things off robs us of the opportunity to accomplish it. Time lost is a loss forever and it cannot be retrieved. Therefore the proverb 'procrastination is the thief of time' is one adage whose words are effective and truthful in real life. If you are punctual at doing things on time or before time, you are a respected member of society. The ability to remain consistent with your choice is a proficiency that necessitates a lot of will-power. Choosing not to procrastinate requires exceptional principles, self-discipline and vigorous determination of the mind. One who does not procrastinate will be more successful in life emotionally, physically and mentally.

An employee who reports to work on time and does not adjourn doing things will have an enhanced chance of being promoted than the ones who does procrastinate. Life offers you many opportunities and we must seize them before they disappear into the midst of lost opportunities. Procrastination is your enemy as it is the stealer of your time. By procrastinating, you are letting time slip past your very eyes and doing nothing about it. Procrastination is the thief of time because it steals away the beauty of what time brings to you. Time is a rigid conception of life for human beings, something that is immune to your system. The robber of time is most definitely procrastination.

My advice is to never do tomorrow what you can do today. You can't start the next chapter of your life if you keep re-reading the last one. The best way to get something done is to begin. Do not wait; the time will never be just right to do what you plan to do. Start where you are, and work with whatever tools you have, and better tools will be found as you progress along the way. Every second is a chance to turn your life around for good. You don't always get what you wish for, but you get what you work for.

Track Your Achievements

A number of people have posted about Ben Franklin's virtues, which is one of the coolest ideas for tracking your habits. I've thought about this idea for quite some time, and just some months back I decided to twist it to fit my own goals. I created a simple spreadsheet for tracking my habits and goals, from being a world class author to my savings goals. Now, I have a weekly schedule worked out so that each of these is scheduled for different days, so on this chart I have the other days grayed out when I don't need to worry about that goal or habit. So here is the key: each evening, I review my day (as Ben Franklin did). I look through the boxes for that day, and put a dot for the achievement or goals I accomplished for that day, and an "x" for those I didn't. My goal is to have all dots and no "x"s. Then, I look at what's coming up for the next day, so I am prepared for tomorrow. I do this review as the last thing I do before going to bed. It has been working like a charm. Like any system, it only works if you work it, but so far I've been working it. I highly recommend this system, as it's a great way not only to track your achievement and goals, but to motivate yourself to stick with them each day.

I expect that you have heard this before. Yes, it can be an effort but if you are truly struggling with your finances this does make a difference. Just like keeping a food diary does for those who want to lose weight. Most people are unconscious about how they spend their money. They honestly don't know where it goes. It is easy to track the big ticket and consistent items (rent/mortgage, insurance, food, going out to eat etc.). The miscellaneous expenditures add up. Part of the reason is that I have been told that once you have kids, your money just evaporates. I will soon be having my first child so I am interested in seeing how this occurs and what I can do about it. I cannot tell you how many times friends have presented their budget to me and it shows they should be saving a large sum of money. I ask if they are saving anything and the answer is nothing or much less than what their budget says they should be saving. So money is going towards things that are not listed on that budget. The way to get answers is to track your spending and go back and see what you actually spent money on over the past year.

There are various ways to track your achievements:

- Paper and pencil with a notebook or spreadsheet for recording them;
- Online tools like mint.com could be of help;
- Software like Quicken or MoneyDance is useful.

The important thing is just to do it. The only way to fix this is to take the time and effort to follow up your achievement in detail. Congratulate yourself on each achievement. What you achieve today should gear you up to greater heights in your exploit to financial dominion. As a financial planner I believe cash flow is one area that is not given enough attention when it comes to using your resources to aid your achievement in life. This may be due to the fact that it is challenging for an advisor to provide assistance with it since spending is such a personal decision and outside an advisor's control. I do not mean to present this as something that is easy to do. It is not. We all have our own deeply established habits and beliefs around money so be patient with yourself. Your cash flow is the key to financial success or achieving financial independence. So start right now. Take some actions now to get your cash flow and savings moving in the right direction.

Don't Hold on Your Negative Past

Don't let the past hold you back. This aspect talks more of your negative past. Definitely, sometimes you may fall short of your expectation, that doesn't translate to be the end of the world for you; rather you should put on the guard of courage and move on with life. While positive past is a good reminiscence on which to build extra energy for the future, negative past contributes nothing to your well-being than to stop your progress. The only part of the past you should hold on is your good memories that can keep you better prepared for your next level encounter in life. When you hold on the past, you are missing the present. What you did yesterday brought you to where you are today; and it cannot be altered anymore. We hold ourselves back in ways both big and small, by lacking self-confidence and believe in ourselves. What you do with today is what determines your tomorrow. Therefore, it is better to work with the present than being tied to the past. The greatest wisdom is to embrace your mistakes, and seek for ways to correct them. Some of the things that we hold on to the most, are the things that we need to let go. Anyhow you think it; you know you can't go on living everyday in the past. If you don't detach yourself from your past, you may pass away with it. Say good bye to what's behind you. Some people think that to be strong is to never feel pain. However, the strongest people are the ones who have felt pain, understood it, accepted it and learned from it. Don't tie down your future because you're too busy holding on to your past.

Never Accept Defeat and Never Give-up

Most people quickly get overthrown by the force of defeat, and therefore give up. "*I haven't failed. I've found 10,000 ways that don't work.*" This statement was from Thomas Edison, the inventor of the first commercial light bulb. If you have a goal of what you have set to achieve, keep up with the vision. It is something obvious, that each passing day that do not produce positive energy towards achieving your goal can bring frustration your way; I will advice you don't give up. It is an exceptional thing in life to take a leap at success of any kind the first time and achieve it.

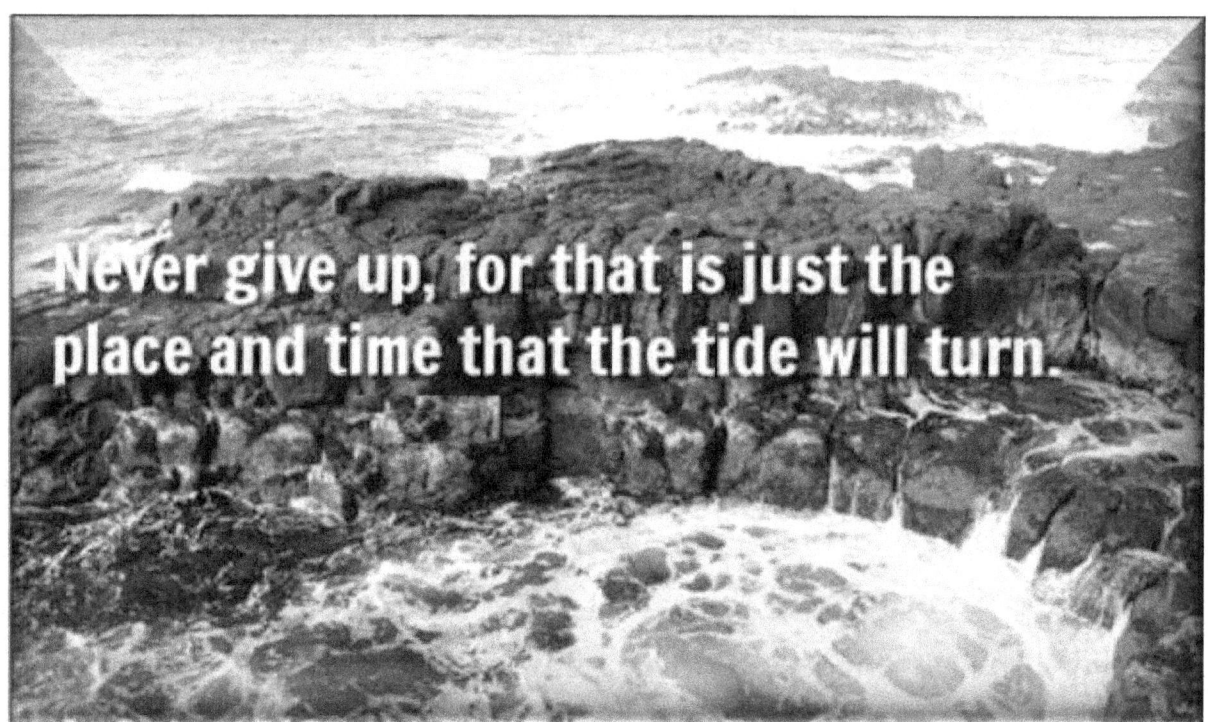

Cars and airplanes are two important and very useful discoveries of our time today. If you get to know the number of times the inventors of these valuable assets had failed before these things came into existence, you will be overwhelmed. But rather than allow the force of defeat to overtake them, each failed attempt is seen as one of the many ways that things should not be done. So they retrace their steps and start all over. Those failed attempts have added to your experience in that area of endeavor, and therefore teaches you not to go in that direction anymore. If you don't accept defeat, for sure you will not give up.

About the Author

Victor Peters is a motivational speaker and an ardent practitioner of self–improvement techniques with many years of experience in human capacity building and personal development. He has conducted training to organizations and individuals on personal development and self–improvement. After many years of studying, practicing and gaining practical experience, he decided to share the knowledge and experience he has gained, through his blog, and frequent writings in journals and other book publishing media.

Victor holds a Bachelor of Science (BSc) degree in Computer Science from the University of Wollongong Australia, a Master of Science (MSc) and Doctor of Philosophy (PhD) degree, also in Computer Science from Universiti Malaysia Sarawak (UNIMAS).

Victor Peters is the author of several books, among which are 'Find and Never Lose It', 'Is this Luck or Deliberate Working?', 'Financial Success Tool Kit', Financial Worries? Try This! Power of Thought and Action on your Mind; Financial Wisdom in the Days of Small Beginning; Developing and Spreading your Financial Tentacles; and 'How Best to Tame the Vindictive Monster called Poverty'.